£6-95

THE DAVID HUME INSTITUTE
THE SUNTORY-TOYOTA INTERNATIONAL CENTRE FOR ECONOMICS AND RELATED DISCIPLINES,
LONDON SCHOOL OF ECONOMICS AND POLITICAL SCIENCE

# STUDENT LOANS: THE NEXT STEPS

To the Outsiders who should be Insiders

THE DAVID HUME INSTITUTE
THE SUNTORY-TOYOTA INTERNATIONAL CENTRE FOR
ECONOMICS AND RELATED DISCIPLINES,
LONDON SCHOOL OF ECONOMICS AND POLITICAL SCIENCE

# STUDENT LOANS: THE NEXT STEPS

Nicholas Barr

ABERDEEN UNIVERSITY PRESS

First published 1989
Aberdeen University Press
A member of the Pergamon Group



**British Library Cataloguing in Publication Data**
Barr, N A (Nicholas Adrian), *1943–*
Student Loans: the next steps.
1. Great Britain. Higher education institutions.
Students. Financial assistance. Loans from government
I. Title
378′.362

ISBN 0 08 037966 4

PRINTED IN GREAT BRITAIN
THE UNIVERSITY PRESS
ABERDEEN

# Foreword

In September 1988, The David Hume Institute (DHI) and the Suntory-Toyota International Centre for Economics and Related Disciplines (ST/ICERD), London School of Economics and Political Science co-operated in the publication of *Strategies for Higher Education* by John Barnes and Nicholas Barr, David Hume Paper No. 10, Aberdeen University Press. The impact of this work on the debate concerning higher education finance has been considerable, and one particular feature of that debate has been the strong criticism of the Government's proposals for student loan finance (*Top-Up Loans for Students*, Cm. 520, London HMSO, 1988). An introduction to the loan finance issue is to be found in David Hume Paper No. 10, but within a general framework of university financing. This new Paper by one of the authors is a detailed critique of the Government's position, coupled with constructive proposals for what he regards as a much more sensible system of loan finance.

Neither DHI nor ST/ICERD has a collective view on any policy matter and therefore Dr Barr is solely responsible for the views expressed in his Paper. However, both institutions are glad to have this further opportunity to co-operate in the publication of these proposals on university finance. Dr Barr's work is in the best traditions of British policy analysis in economics combining as he does a thorough exposition of the principles governing student financing with a tract for the times.

Alan Peacock
Executive Editor
The David Hume Institute

Nicholas Stern
Professor of Economics
London School of Economics and
Chairman ST/ICERD

# Contents

# Figures and Tables

# Preface

This is the story of a good idea in a naughty world. The good idea was Mervyn King's—that student loans should be repaid via the National Insurance system. The naughty world is full of intrigue and political skulduggery. All life is there—there are the goodies (the Department of Education and Science) who want expansion, and the baddies (the Treasury) who do not; and there are other attractions like the Committee of Vice-Chancellors and Principals (CVCP) and the Association of University Teachers, locked in mortal combat over salaries whilst more important matters, such as student loans and the consequences of the Education Reform Act, are left largely unattended.

Though student loans are at the centre of a much wider debate about the future of higher education, the idea is anything but new. Early proposals in the UK literature for loans with income-related repayments were by Peacock and Wiseman (1964), Prest (1966), Blaug (1966) and Glennerster, Merrett and Wilson (1968). The 1960s debate is summarised by Blaug (1970, pp 293–307), and Robbins' conversion to this type of loan in Robbins (1980) (though the actual conversion was earlier).

My first debt, therefore, is to the dauntingly eminent people who paved the way. Since virtually all of them (Blaug, Glennerster, Merrett, Peacock, Prest, Robbins, Wilson and Wiseman) were or are at the London School of Economics (LSE) it is fitting that many at the School, individually and collectively, have contributed both to the current debate and to this book.

Much of the present ferment of ideas is attributable to the controversy engendered by the passage through Parliament of the Education Reform Bill (as it then was). Many of us at the LSE were strongly opposed to the centralising tendency implied by such institutions as the Universities Funding Council and its equivalent body for polytechnics and colleges. It became clear that institutions of higher education could become more free to run themselves only if they became less dependent on Treasury funding. Various contributions have been lobbed into the arena, including those by Kedourie (1988), Barnes and Barr (1988) and various (unpublished) reports for the CVCP. Giving students access to funding over and above that from the maintenance grant and parental contributions is part of that trend.

But student loans arise also out of the manifest problems of the current UK system of tax-funded maintenance grants: the grant is too low; parental contributions work very badly; the system is expensive and hence is a major contributory cause of the fact that the UK has the smallest higher-education sector of any advanced industrialised country.

This book is part of that wider debate on higher education. Earlier versions, both before and after the publication of the White Paper on student loans (UK, 1988), were sent to Robert Jackson, the Minister for Higher Education, to argue for a system of student loans that makes a major contribution to expansion and improved access. It is appropriate to thank him. We come from different political backgrounds, and have disagreed strongly for much of the time; but the disagreement has always been of the constructive sort which leads to new ideas and refinement of old ones. That the scheme has improved over the months is partly due to him.

My debts are many and great. The LSE's Suntory-Toyota International Centre for Economics and Related Disciplines (ST/ICERD) has provided practical help and encouragement, and facilitated the venture at every turn, most particularly by funding a conference on higher education at the LSE in September 1988. I am grateful to Professor Nicholas Stern, the Chairman of ST/ICERD, and Professor Sir Alan Peacock, the Executive Director of the David Hume Institute, for their continued support and encouragement in producing this companion piece to last year's collaboration, with John Barnes, between the two institutions. My thanks also to the Geography Department Drawing Office at LSE who produced the diagrams.

The specific origin of the scheme set out here was a conversation about student loans with Mervyn King in July 1988, when he suggested the use of the National Insurance mechanism as a natural way to collect repayments. My greatest debt of all is therefore to him for providing an idea of such strength that it provides the firmest of foundations for what is built upon it in Chapter 5.

My companions-in-arms, John Barnes and Iain Crawford have spent many hours discussing these matters with me. John Barnes read earlier versions, and repeatedly stressed the importance of private-sector funds. The analysis in Chapter 4 is very much Iain Crawford's property; and his is the political nous which has kept the National Insurance idea in play despite an initial lack of enthusiasm in government. Chapter 5 includes an inspired idea of Rory O'Driscoll's that a bank's entitlement to a share of the yield of graduates' National Insurance Contributions is a saleable financial asset, i.e. that there could be a secondary market in student loans. I owe a major debt also to Mark Blaug for the time and care he has devoted to guiding a novice through the economics of education literature.

Many others have been very generous with their time, their ideas and their comments since Barnes and Barr went to press in September 1988, including Meghnad Desai, John Flemming, Lucien Foldes, Howard Glennerster, Gervas Huxley, Tom Nossiter, Mark Robson and David Walker. I am grateful for their help, and for the encouragement and support from colleagues across the political spectrum and (though I would not embarrass them by naming them) by politicians of all parties.

I am grateful also for the education I received from participants at conferences on Student Loans at the Institute of Education, and on the

Future Funding and Management of Higher Education at the LSE, both in September 1988, and at the Canada-UK Colloquium in Mississauga, Ontario in November 1988. Many students have helped by exuberantly pointing out flaws in earlier versions; arguing with them has forced me to think more clearly, as also have questions and comments at numerous seminars and debates.

Preparing this book for publication has been rather hasty, since it has been written to a policy rather than an academic deadline. Readers will, I hope, forgive any rough edges. Errors, of course, remain my responsibility.

Finally, a word of reminder of what this is all about. It is to expand higher education and improve opportunities, above all for those many people outside the higher education system, young and not-so-young, who ought to be inside. It is to them that this book is dedicated.

Nicholas Barr
London
March 1989

The major resource in all human societies is human productive capacity . . . human capital as it has come to be called
(Friedman, 1976, p 4)

# 1 The Aims of Policy

## 1.1 The Backdrop

Student support in Britain has been a political hot potato for much of the 1980s. Sir Keith Joseph (as he then was) introduced a Green Paper in 1985 (UK, 1985), and suggested during the accompanying discussion that not only the maintenance grant but also student fees should be means tested on parental income. The scheme sank without trace. It foundered on the rocks of Tory backbenchers, who deserted the scheme in droves once they realised the ferocity of middle-class parents threatened with the loss of one of their perks. A clear political lesson is that reform of student maintenance should not impose extra burdens on parents, a conclusion supported by the economic analysis in Chapters 2 and 3.

The current canter round the houses began in June 1986 when Kenneth Baker, Sir Keith Joseph's successor as Secretary of State for Education and Science, set up a review of student support. A year later, the Conservative election manifesto said:

> The purpose of the review is to improve the overall prospect of students so that *more are encouraged to enter higher education.* No final conclusions have been reached, but we believe that top-up loans to supplement grants are one way, among others, of bringing in new finance to help students and *relieve pressure on their parents* (Conservative Party, 1987, p 22, my emphasis).

Note the italicised phrases: the first gives support to the aim of access and hence also to expansion (since access cannot be improved without additional places in higher education); the second shows a keen awareness of the lessons of 1985.

A White Paper (UK, 1988) was finally published with minimal fanfare on the day after the US Presidential election, ensuring that discussion and press coverage were, to say the least, muted. Though formally a White Paper, it was the greenest White Paper most commentators had seen, leaving major parts of the scheme, most crucially the repayment mechanism, for later decision. A consultation period to 1 February 1989 was announced, during which many groups submitted evidence to the Department of Education and Science (DES).

This book is a revised version of one of those submissions. Its purpose was to convince the government that the White Paper proposals were in important respects deficient, and that an alternative set of arrangements would be greatly superior in terms of equity to students and in terms of the resources they saved—resources which could be used to expand higher education. The purpose of this book is to explain why it is right that student maintenance should in part be through a system of loans, but that it is absolutely crucial that it should be the *right* system of loans.

Many readers will question why loans of any sort are necessary. They will argue that access to education is a right; that education is not merely a matter of training people for the job market, but something worthwhile for its own sake; and that languages, literature and music are as important as 'useful' subjects like engineering. Those value judgements I share wholeheartedly. But their proponents serve their cause ill if they ignore the fact that higher eduction is *also* an economic commodity. It is a common confusion to argue that because something is a right it should be free, as is medical care under the National Health Service. But food, equally, is a right; and yet we pay for it at Sainsburys and Tescos and nobody argues that there is anything wrong about doing so (for a defence of the NHS (and of private markets for food), see Barr, 1987, Chs 12 and 13).

Economics is called the dismal science because it continually reminds us that resources are finite and so, if used for one purpose, cannot be used for another. Higher education cannot escape that reality. Resources devoted to universities and polytechnics are at the expense of other activities: there is (and will always be) a queue which includes pensioners, the unemployed and disabled, the NHS and pre-university education, quite apart from private consumption. Ignoring these painful choices, to put it bluntly, is selling future generations of students down the river. It is precisely to avoid that happening that this book deliberately sets out the issues in economic terms.

This chapter discusses the aims of higher education policy, since alternative systems of student support should be judged by the extent to which they contribute to their achievement. Section 2 (which can be skipped by those primarily interested in policy) sets out the main theoretical arguments; section 3 establishes the main policy aims as access and expansion. The concluding section brings out what, with hindsight, has been a crucial aspect of the debate—the existence of a major conflict within government as to what the aims of higher education policy should be.

Chapters 2 and 3 discuss the lessons to be learned from experience in the UK and elsewhere, with particular emphasis on solutions which do not work. Chapter 2 rules out an expansion of the present system through increased tax-funded maintenance and increased support from parents. Chapter 3 looks at various badly-designed loan schemes elsewhere, and concludes that loans organised like mortgages or bank loans would actively hinder expansion and access.

Chapter 4 looks at a specific non-solution—the 1988 White Paper, which suggests that students should be partly supported by a loan from Treasury funds, with repayments collected by the banking system. Not only does the White Paper fail to foster expansion and improved access; it fails even in its own terms to save any public resources at all.

Chapter 5 sets out an alternative proposal, in which students borrow from banks, and repayments are collected by employers in the form of a small addition to graduates' National Insurance Contributions. The scheme is fair (not least because repayments are strictly related to the individual student's subsequent income); it is administratively cheap (because it is 'piggy backed' onto an existing administrative system); and it yields savings so large that they allow higher education to expand in the 1990s and *in addition* allow Treasury savings after about 2005, when the adverse demographic prospects start to take effect. The scheme, in short, makes a major contribution to expansion and access, and does so without *any* increase in public spending. The main thrust of the argument and details of the scheme are summarised in Chapter 6. Readers in a hurry can get the main arguments by reading sections 3 and 4 of this chapter and then proceeding to Chapter 6.

## 1.2 The Aims of Higher Education 1: Theory

This section discusses the broad aims of efficiency and equity; the next turns to what they might mean in practice. Economic efficiency has a number of dimensions, of which three are particularly important: the *quantity* dimension relates to the optimal size of the higher-education sector; *quality* relates to the type of higher education. A different concept, *X-efficiency,* relates to the effectiveness with which resources are used. These concepts are discussed in more detail in Barr (1987, pp 71–4) and the references therein.

### *The Quantity of Higher Education*

The issue concerns what elsewhere (Barr, 1987, p 326) I have called *macro efficiency*, i.e. what proportion of national resources should be devoted to higher education. This aspect focuses on the net benefits of higher education in comparison with other activities. In principle, investment should proceed to the point where the marginal social return (both in static terms and in terms of future economic growth, and including non-monetary benefits) equals the return the resources involved could make if devoted to some other activity. The optimal size of the sector should take account of any external benefits, i.e. the extent to which higher education confers benefits on people other than the individual recipient.

Is the efficient size of the sector larger than currently? First, is there an investment argument for expanding higher education, i.e. would expansion increase the rate of economic growth? Second, and separately, should there be expansion for consumption reasons, i.e. would extra resources add sufficient to the quality of life (for reasons other than output growth) to make such expansion efficient?

**Higher education as an investment good** Several arguments are made for expanding the system. International competitive pressures are increasing, a process which will accelerate after 1992. The living standard of any country whose productivity lags will decline relative to that in other countries. The requirement, therefore, is to raise the productivity of capital and labour; if higher education contributes to productivity there is an efficiency case for expansion.

A second argument relates to the demographic prospects. The proportion of elderly people is rising, presaging high costs of pensions and health care. Thus, it is argued, we should cut all other forms of public spending. In important respects, this argument is false (see Barr, 1987, Ch 9). The issue here is not a short-run inflationary crisis in which both current *and* capital spending are cut (e.g. the stringency of the 1980–1 period), but a long-term issue of output growth. The efficient response to a decline in the number of workers is to increase the capital:labour ratio. This implies cutting consumption today, so as to release resources for investment in technology *and* in human capital, both of which will increase output in the future. There might be a case for cutting public and private consumption, but none whatever for cutting productive investment in either sector. Demographic change means that we need a highly skilled labour force within the next decade. Expansion, it can be argued, is therefore necessary precisely *because* demographic prospects are an argument for additional investment in labour productivity.

A third factor is technological advance, leading to rising demand for skilled people and declining demand for the unskilled. The resulting changes are a shift towards the so-called 'knowledge-based society'; they also underlie the debate about whether or not there is a growing 'underclass' (see Dahrendorf, 1988, Chs 7 and 8). The argument, however, is not a simple one. Technological progress increases the demand for skilled labour; but in specific areas it can decrease it, e.g. computers are much more 'user friendly' than they were 25 years ago. However, the development of sophisticated technology needs a substantially educated population: it can hardly be an accident that Silicone Valley (in both its California and Massachussetts manifestations) grew up in an area with many universities. The *use* of modern technology also requires skills; and its rate of change requires individuals with skills which are flexible enough to adapt to changing technology.

All three arguments create a strong efficiency presumption for increasing the volume of resources devoted to higher education. Amazingly, though, it is not possible to offer definitive, quantitative *proof*. It is worth explaining why.

**The screening hypothesis** The efficiency case for expansion rests on the argument that higher education is *causally* related to increased productivity. In contrast, the so-called screening hypothesis argues that education is *associated* with increased productivity, but does not cause it (Spence, 1973; Layard and Walters, 1978, pp 386–9; Varian, 1984, Ch 8; and, for a compendious survey of this and other aspects, Blaug, 1976).

The argument starts by observing that the distribution of earnings is the result of a complex interaction of factors including sex, race, family circumstances, natural ability and the quantity and quality of education (Blaug, 1970, pp 32–46). The screening hypothesis is a special case which argues that education beyond a basic level does not increase individual productivity. Instead, it is assumed at its simplest that firms seek high-ability workers but are unable, prior to employing them, to distinguish them from those with low ability. The problem is one of asymmetric information (i.e. the individual worker knows more about his/her productivity than does the prospective employer); the problem is analytically identical to that of adverse selection in insurance markets, or more generally of 'lemons' (Akerlof, 1970).

Individuals therefore have an incentive to make themselves distinctive by some sort of signal. According to the screening hypothesis higher education fills exactly this function. By and large it is high-ability individuals who perform well in the educational system. Educational achievement is therefore correlated with higher productivity but does not cause it, and hence is no more than a screening or signalling device to prospective employers, which it is in the *individual's* (though not necessarily in society's) interests to acquire. Just as an individual's good health may be due more to a naturally strong constitution than to medical care so, according to this view, is productivity the result of natural ability rather than post-primary education.

The screening hypothesis, at its strongest, argues that higher education does nothing to increase individual productivity and has no economic value at all. There are at least three counter-arguments. First, even without empirical evidence the proposition in that form can be rejected. In the case of specific skills such as medicine, higher education clearly makes a direct contribution to individual skills; the same is true of architecture and many forms of science; and how many economists did the Government Economic Service employ 25 years ago?

The second problem with the screening hypothesis is that it assumes that there is only one type of job. In practice skills and job characteristics are both heterogeneous, so that it is necessary to match workers and jobs. Even if education were only a screen (which we have just seen is not the case), its social return as a matching device is likely to be positive.

A third argument recognises the international dimension. If employers insist (whether rightly or not) that graduates are necessary for some jobs, then a shortage of UK graduates could drive them to expand their operations overseas. Just as Nissan, in making a choice between Britain and other EC countries, seeks labour of a certain type so, for example, will financial institutions locate in countries with sufficient graduates of the right type. This argument is valid even if the screening hypothesis is true. Given the single European market and the global village, Britain simply cannot afford to opt out.

Whether there is *some* validity in the hypothesis, and to what extent, is an empirical matter; the verdict is undecided and, given the intractable problems of testing the hypothesis, likely to remain so. The overriding problem is that we cannot measure quantitatively the effect of higher education on individual productivity, because we cannot measure all the relevant variables. The determinants of individual productivity include measurable attributes like sex, race and educational qualifications; they also include vital but utterly unmeasurable factors like natural ability and the influence of family background. Statistical analysis which attempts to quantify the effects of the former without including the latter faces serious technical problems, and results based on it cannot wholly be relied on.[1]

**The case for expansion,** though strong in presumptive terms, therefore needs to be made with care. The screening hypothesis at its strongest cannot be true, but it is not possible to show whether it is partially true. Thus we know that higher education on average *does* increase individual productivity, but we cannot measure the extent of that increase. The fact that we cannot say *how much* additional investment there should be, should not, however, obscure the underlying case for expansion.

A second investment argument is that higher education offers a hedge against technological dynamism. Specific skills may become redundant in the face of technological progress, but higher education gives people *general* skills, and so is an investment which saves the resources which would otherwise have to be devoted to retraining labour whose skills had become redundant.

A related argument is that higher education can have cumulative effects. It is argued (not least by the present government) that income redistribution requires higher taxation; and if the resulting labour-supply effects reduce labour productivity the cumulative results over time can be major (the state of the UK economy in the late 1970s is frequently cited). But exactly the same argument can be applied to under-investment in education. Alfred Marshall, writing 100 years ago argued that:

> [T]hey [the children of the working class] go to the grave carrying undeveloped abilities and faculties; which if they could have borne full fruit would have added to the material wealth of the country . . . to say nothing of higher considerations . . . many times as much as would have covered the expense of providing adequate opportunities for their development.
>
> *But the point we have especially to insist now is that the evil is cumulative.* The worse fed are the children of one generation, the less will they earn when they grow up, and the less will be their power of providing adequately for . . . their children; and so on to the following generations (Marshall, 1961, Book VI, p 569, my emphasis).

Marshall, of course, was writing about school education. But the quote brings out a key point—the high costs of making the wrong investment decisions, given their cumulative impact. The costs of not expanding higher education when we should expand are likely to be much greater than the costs of expansion which turns out not to have been strictly necessary.

Higher education can also be viewed as a consumption good. It is rationed in the UK more stringently than in any other industrialised country; and there is ample evidence that the demand for places exceeds the supply. The demonstrable existence of potential students prepared to pay for higher education (net of any external benefits thereby created) are an additional argument for expansion.

### *The Quality and Type of Higher Education*

The issue here is one of *micro efficiency*, which is concerned with the net benefits of different types of higher education (e.g. subject mix). The key issue is consumer sovereignty, i.e. are choices made more efficiently in a decentralised, market-oriented system or should higher education be largely centrally planned?

In discussing consumer choice, account must be taken of four sets of actors who seek to maximise utility/profit—either their own, or that of others: students, teachers and others in higher education, employers, and government. So far as students are concerned there are two central questions: do they have sufficient information to choose rationally; and what price should they pay (i.e. to what extent should higher education be subsidised)?

**Students as informed consumers** The issue of individual choice versus manpower planning in higher education is one of the main topics in Barnes and Barr (1988). The debate has two dimensions. The first is ideological: it is about whether or not one supports liberal educational values, consumer choice and education as something of value in its own right, not merely as an instrument of economic growth. The second part is technical: are students as consumers likely to make good choices; and would central planners be able to make better choices? Put another way, are students capable of choosing degrees and institutions in a way which maximises their personal satisfaction; and do their choices make the greatest contribution to national goals such as output growth?

So far as the first is concerned, students' ability to make sensible choices is controversial. The theoretical issue is whether or not they have sufficient information to choose rationally. It should be remembered, first, that students make choices already; and the quality of those choices could be improved if more (and more systematic) information were available not just on factual matters (e.g. the content of a degree) but also on quality (e.g. of teaching).

A strong measure of consumer sovereignty is defensible for two theoretical reasons: the student has time to acquire the information he/she needs and time to seek advice; and the information is sufficiently simple for the student to be able to understand it and, to a large extent, evaluate it (for detailed discussion of the relevant economic theory, see Barr, 1987, Ch 4). It cannot be taken for granted that these conditions will always hold: they largely fail in the case of medical care, and also for much school education; but (though I have no evidence beyond casual empiricism) they hold to a very large extent in the case of higher education, where students are an intelligent and fairly 'street-wise' consumer group.

Turning to the needs of the economy, do students make better choices than central planners? All the evidence is that they do. Research connected with the Robbins Report (UK, 1963) showed the difficulty of trying to project the nation's medium-term manpower needs (Moser and Layard, 1964; Blaug, 1967; Layard, 1972).

Most experts therefore agree that central planning of higher education is counter-productive in both ideological and technical terms. This conclusion in no way denies governments a right to views about and influence over the direction of higher education; it merely denies the efficacy of *excessive* government intervention.

**The efficiency role of subsidies** The issue of efficient student choice thus depends on the quality of the information they have; it also depends on whether or not they face an efficient price. The analytical issue is whether or not there is an *efficiency* case for subsidising higher education. External benefits (i.e. benefits to individuals other than those directly concerned) can arise in several ways. First, if higher education raises a student's earnings, it increases his future tax payments; in the absence of any subsidy, his investment in a degree would confer a 'dividend' on taxpayers in the future. Quite apart from equity issues, this would be inefficient, and is therefore the minimum case for a subsidy.

It is part of the conventional wisdom that higher education also creates more general external benefits (Le Grand and Robinson, 1984, pp 64–6; Barr, 1987, pp 291–2). *Production benefits* arise if education not only makes an individual more productive, but also contributes to the productivity of others (e.g. if colleagues learn the same word processing package they contribute to each others' productivity as well as to their own). *Cultural benefits* are those arising out of shared experiences and common values (including a shared belief that differences in opinion are to be welcomed).

However, there are arguments in the opposite direction. Higher education encourages questioning attitudes and so, it might be argued, can create negative cultural benefits (Grosvenor Square, Paris and Berkeley in 1968 have been cited as examples). In addition, if higher education raises expectations excessively the result, it is sometimes suggested, is individuals who are discontented with their job; if this lowers not only individual utility but also productivity, production benefits can also be negative.

The arguments in the previous paragraph are intended merely as a caution against blindly *assuming* that higher education creates external benefits. If there are potential costs as well as benefits, the issue must be resolved empirically. Again, intractable measurement problems make definitive answer impossible. The heart of the difficulty is that education may not simply raise an individual's earnings (which can be measured) but also his/her job satisfaction and enjoyment of life generally (which cannot).[2] Thus any attempt to measure the private rate of return to education is highly suspect because, of necessity, non-monetary returns are omitted. Estimates of the social rate of return are doubly suspect: they omit non-monetary factors and (since no other procedure is possible) they also ignore the possibility of screening.

Thus there is a strong presumption that higher education creates external benefits; and because of the 'tax dividend' an unarguable efficiency case exists for subsidy, though it is not possible to quantify its optimal size.

**The role of institutions** Alongside students, employers and government, the fourth set of actors are teachers and others in higher education. In the standard competitive model a firm makes a profit-maximising quantity of a homogeneous product which is sold to consumers, who can choose to buy from competing suppliers. That model does not fit higher education well. First, institutions are not profit maximising. Second, they do not offer a standard product identical to that offered by competing institutions. Third, it is not clear what the 'product' is; it has many dimensions, whose relative importance will vary from student to student. Fourth, the 'product' is in many cases an indirect one. Employers do not buy an LSE degree; they hire an LSE graduate who has multiple characteristics, some (but by no means all) related to his/her degree.

The theory of non-profit maximising institutions is not well developed.[3] Since it is not possible to quantify a university's output, it is not possible either to measure the institution's efficiency. What can be said, however, is that both theory and empirical evidence argue against seeking efficiency through central planning (Barnes and Barr, 1988, Ch 2). The core argument is that central monitoring of university activities requires a large amount of detailed information: and that information is (a) costly to acquire, (b) can in many cases not be measured, and (c) is often subverted by the individuals supplying it to the central planning authority. A degree of competition will make institutions more efficient, even if the effect cannot be measured.

The conclusion (albeit a controversial one) is that consumer choice and competition should play a major role, though modified by public policy as described in Barnes and Barr (1988, Ch 6). Consumer choice, it is argued there, is the least bad way of representing the interests of students; it is also more effective than central planning at meeting the needs of employers, whose demands are an ingredient in students' decisions. Competition between universities brings about a meeting ground between the needs of students, those of employers and those of teachers and others in higher education. It makes universities responsive to student and employer demand, but gives them freedom to innovate.

A major implication, if the system is indeed to be competitive, and not dominated by government, is that there should be plural sources of funding, so that no one group of actors has overriding influence; and part of the funding should be channelled via individual students, so as to enhance their power as consumers.

**X-efficiency** is concerned with using resources as effectively as possible. Again, competition contributes to this aim. Excessive planning is administratively costly. Centrally-planned systems are generally publicly funded; and universities' use of such public funds may or may not be subject to scrutiny. Without scrutiny, inefficiency, though not inevitable, is likely;

but if there is scrutiny, the information requirements are large and will be much more costly than under a decentralised system.

### *Equity*

Equity is a slippery concept, and the literature is huge (for a cogent discussion, see Le Grand, 1984). I shall define equity to mean equality of opportunity (for detailed discussion, see Barr, 1987, pp 139–42 and 285–7). Equality of opportunity does not mean that everyone gets the same quantity of education (because people differ in their preferences and aptitudes), nor that everyone achieves the same level of educational attainment (which is infeasible). What it does imply is that if individuals A and B have similar tastes and ability, each should receive the same education, irrespective of extraneous considerations like race, sex, social class or parental income. This definition is not foolproof (for instance, it begs the question of the extent to which 'ability' is exogenous or is determined mainly by social conditions). But it is at least workable; and it has the merit that it apportions scarcity in what most people would regard as a just way.

Since 1963 one of the main pillars of higher education policy in Britain has been the so-called 'Robbins Principle' (after the Chairman of the 1963 Royal Commission on Higher Education (UK, 1963)). The Robbins Report 'assumed as an axiom that courses of higher education should be available for all those who are qualified by ability and attainment to pursue them and who wish to do so'. Such an aim is closely related to the definition of equality of opportunity in the previous paragraph. Equality of opportunity is compatible with the Robbins Principle, but is weaker. Unlike the Robbins Principle, it does not guarantee a place for anyone with the desire and aptitude; it merely guarantees that no-one will be excluded on grounds such as parental income or social class.

Both the words *qualified* and *desired* are important. The power of higher education to improve the class-mix of its students is strictly circumscribed. If a student with the necessary qualifications desires to go to university but is rejected for reasons of social class, then access suffers and the fault lies with the higher-education sector. On the other hand, if an intelligent student fails to get into higher education through lack of qualifications, then the problem arises not in the higher-education sector, but in the school system. In short, some access problems are relevant to higher education and some are not, and equity has to include discussion of how resources for education should be divided between higher education and policies to promote access earlier in the educational system.

## 1.3 The Aims of Higher Education 2: Policy

Given this background, three specific policy aspects require discussion: access, expansion and how the costs of higher education should be shared.

**Access** is closely related to equity. It implies that student support should be organised so that no-one is prevented by lack of current income from entering higher education. Equally, it means that there should be no substantial class bias in the student composition. It also means that no qualified student who desires to go into higher education should be denied a place.

Improving access is vital. The UK has the smallest higher-education sector of any developed economy (UK, 1988, Chart F). Even allowing for definitional problems and differences in the way the data are compiled, the proportion of UK young people entering higher education is about half that of most of our competitors.

As a result, according to calculations by the Department of Education and Science, something like 19 per cent of qualified applicants are turned away.[4] Even on its own that is a shocking figure: and to that 19 per cent must be added those qualified students who do not apply, and those with the talents to qualify who nevertheless leave school at sixteen. These potential students represent a waste of talent which is unacceptable in both efficiency and equity terms.

**Expansion** can be supported, first, to improve access: with a fixed number of places, access can be increased only through better allocation of existing places; substantial improvement is possible only by having more places. Improvement is partly a matter of equity, to foster equality of opportunity and inter-generational mobility; unequal access also wastes talent.

There is also the argument that higher education should expand for efficiency reasons. The counter-argument is that higher education is only a screening device; that the need, for demographic and other reasons, for skilled people is great, but that higher education makes little contribution to meeting that need; and that the UK, alone among industrialised countries, has withstood the political pressures to overinvest in higher education—pressures which arise because screening does not remove the *private* interests of students to acquire a degree as a signal to employers of their superior productivity.

Because of measurement problems, the case for expansion can never be proved conclusively. But the fact that something (in this case the increased productivity resulting from higher education) cannot be measured does not mean that it does not exist. The argument for expansion remains.

△ In investment terms, the proposition that higher education makes *no* contribution to individual productivity is not tenable. Additional investment in higher education is therefore justifiable, not least because of the demographic prospects.

△ Businesses can increasingly choose in which country to base their operations; thus the size of the British higher-education sector cannot be decided independently of what occurs in other countries.

△ Higher education gives individuals flexible skills, and so offers insurance against rapid changes in technology.

△ The costs of getting things wrong in the direction of underinvestment are much more serious than the reverse.

△ There is a case for expansion of higher education as a consumption good.

△ There is an equity argument for expansion, since improved access is not possible without more places.

Expansion is now official DES policy. In the UK currently, about 14 per cent of the relevant age group go into higher education; Kenneth Baker, in a speech in Lancaster on 5 January 1989, called for an increase to 30 per cent by 2000 ('Baker Calls for College Growth', *Guardian*, 6 January 1989, p 22). The French are currently proposing to increase their age participation rate over the same period to *eighty* per cent ('French Planning to be the Brains of Europe', *Independent*, 19 January 1989, p 9). Even allowing for definitional differences, that is a far cry from 14 per cent.

Unfortunately, the White Paper scheme wholly rules out Kenneth Baker's objective. It proposes that students borrow from Treasury funds. Thus the Treasury pays student fees, the recurrent grant, the maintenance grant and, until repayments come in on a substantial scale, also the loan. According to the White Paper there are no public expenditure savings till 2002; thus there is no prospect of expansion in the short run.

Matters in reality are vastly worse. Chapter 4 shows that the White Paper figures are wholly unrealistic in that they ignore the costs of administration and of the interest subsidy. When the proposals are properly costed they offer no savings at all. Indeed, the scheme *increases* public expenditure, thus ruling out expansion even in the long run.

**Cost sharing** How should the costs of higher education be shared? We know that higher education has three groups of beneficiaries. The students themselves benefit because there is a positive private return to higher education. Industry benefits unambiguously: if the screening hypothesis does not hold, universities make employees more productive; and if it holds in part, higher education benefits employers by giving them useful signals. The third beneficiary is society more generally, represented by the government: higher education creates a 'tax dividend'; and its external effects, though beset by measurement problems, are generally agreed to be positive. Given the beneficiaries, it is efficient that the costs of higher education should be shared between the students, their employers and the taxpayer. This brings us to consideration of student loans, and the general shape they might take.

**Desirable characteristics of a loan scheme** Three characteristics are worth mentioning immediately (the topic is taken up more fully in Chapter 3.4). First, to make expansion easier, the start-up funds should come from the private sector: one source would be the commercial banks; another would be employers. Second, for both efficiency and equity reasons, the loan should be indexed and the interest rate not substantially subsidised. These aspects are discussed in Chapter 3.3.

Third, and crucially, repayments must be related to the student's subsequent income. Lord Robbins, writing in 1980 (p 34) argued that,

> a simple loan system of this sort [i.e. mortgage-type] is subject to very considerable disadvantages, both administrative and moral. A loan system administered in isolation from the general apparatus of public finance is administratively cumbersome and difficult to run. All existing loan systems known to me present obvious difficulties of collection. Even more important are the moral disadvantages. Not all investment in higher education yields a financial return. Under a simple loan scheme some borrowers may overestimate their eventual earning capacity. Some may choose occupations which have a low pecuniary return . . .

Robbins then cites Alan Prest's (1966) proposal for loans with income-related repayments, and goes on to say (*ibid*, p 35) that 'it is a matter of regret to me, personally, that I did not at the time [of the Robbins Report] sufficiently appreciate the advantages of the Prest scheme'.

Nor is this view idiosyncratic. Blaug (1980, p 45) (see also Blaug, 1966) writes that

> virtually every advocate of student loans in Britain (Alan Peacock, Jack Wiseman, Alan Prest, Sir Charles Carter, Gareth Williams, Ernest Rudd, Anthony Flew, Donald Mackay, Michael Crew, Alistair Young, Arthur Seldon, Lord Robbins and Mark Blaug) . . . favours an income-related loans scheme . . .

**The strategy for achieving these aims** is twofold. On the supply side, there should be less public spending on student maintenance, and the public funds thereby released used to increase the number of places in higher education. Though this paper concentrates mainly on how to find the resources for expansion, the demand side is also important. The second leg of the strategy addresses access on the demand side in three ways: by having loans with income-related repayments (so that applicants are not deterred); by offering additional assistance to students in the 16–19 age group (thus improving access at the point where many young people from the lowest socioeconomic groups drop out); and by phasing out the parental contribution, the failure of which is itself a bar to access.

In the scheme suggested in Chapter 5, employers collect loan repayments via the National Insurance Contribution mechanism. This allows secure repayments with minimal default and a low rate of write-off. This security of repayment, crucially, makes it possible for banks to participate. The resulting long-run savings in public expenditure can be as high as £350 million (or even higher if the loan is allowed to exceed half the grant), considerably more than the maximum saving of £230 million claimed by the White Paper (UK, 1988, Annex E). Furthermore, the scheme would result in saving in public expenditure *from the first year*. The scheme thus offers resources for immediate expansion. What is more, the savings are so large (£300 million per year by 2005—see Table 1, line 4) that it is possible to have sustainable expansion in the 1990s *and* net Treasury savings in the early 2000s.

## 1.4 Conflicting Aims

**The Treasury view** The aims in the previous section are those of the DES. They are not the aims of the Treasury. The conflict is summarised in a newspaper article ('Kenneth Baker in Clash with Treasury', *Guardian*, 7 January 1989, p 1) based on a meeting about student loans at the Treasury on 5 January 1989—the same day that Kenneth Baker was making his Lancaster speech.

> Mr Kenneth Baker, the Education Secretary, is locked in a fierce battle with the Treasury for control of higher education, particularly over his plans to ensure a doubling in the numbers of young people going to university or polytechnic by the year 2000.
>
> The Treasury wants to control any future expansion of higher education from the centre, as part of a manpower planning exercise to relate the number of students to the future needs of the economy. But Mr Baker and his ministerial colleagues want a more flexible, market-led system.
>
> These arguments lay behind Mr Baker's call this week for an . . . expansion of higher education . . .

The debate is stark: it is about nothing less than the Robbins Principle. The Treasury (or at least some Treasury officials) takes the view that the size of the higher-education sector and the choice of subject studied, far from being determined by students (i.e. a demand-led system), should be amenable to Treasury control in the light of the nation's need for skilled personnel (i.e. a manpower-planning approach).

There is further evidence for this view. In early November 1988 there was a leak of confidential papers written by Robert Jackson the previous July for a meeting with departmental colleagues. Press coverage at the time of the leak concentrated on a speculative proposal in one of the papers to allow universities to charge extra fees, and rather missed the main point—namely the evidence in the papers of the Treasury view of higher education. One of the papers said:

> Since Robbins the basic principle which the Government has followed with regard to the overall number of students it wishes to support has been that the government will fund places for all would-be students who have the qualifications, and the ability to benefit from higher education.
>
> . . .[T]he Treasury insisted that the principle of accommodating student demand should be qualified . . . by an inter-departmental review of the need for highly qualified manpower. This review . . . could lead the Government, for the first time since Robbins, to formulate a policy on the overall numbers of

> students it wants to fund, independently of demand. *If it does so, this piece of 'manpower planning' will have been driven by the Treasury . . .*
>
> Our position in this matter should continue, I believe, to be that the Government should fund student demand as it arises. (Robert Jackson's leaked private papers, 25 July 1988, my emphasis).

The importance of the interdepartmental conflict (made utterly clear by the italicised sentence in the middle paragraph of the quotation) cannot be overstated: the DES favour access and expansion and hence continued adherence to the Robbins view of higher education; the Treasury, it appears, want to recant on the Robbins Principle. The issue is therefore much more than the ostensible debate, about what is the best sort of loan scheme. It is a debate about the whole nature of higher education.

**Implications for the White Paper** It is only against this background that the White Paper can fully be understood. What should have been a straightforward task took $2\frac{1}{2}$ years, and the result (as argued in Chapter 4) was a dog's breakfast. The reason is clear: the White Paper was written to bring about access and expansion *and* central control and manpower planning. These objectives are utterly incompatible: the Archangel Gabriel could not write a coherent White Paper to achieve them. It is therefore not surprising that the White Paper was late and lacking coherence; its writers were set an impossible task, and the heavy criticism in Chapter 4 should be read in that light. A further White Paper on Higher Education foreshadowed for later in the year may shed some light on how the battle is progressing.

# 2 Non-Solution 1: Lessons from Britain

This chapter starts with a brief discussion of the main problems of British higher education as a whole. Section 2 looks at problems specific to student support, and section 3 argues that expansion of the present system of student maintenance, far from contributing to expansion and access, is likely to do the reverse.

## 2.1 Problems with the System of Higher Education

The organisation of higher education in Britain has two main problems: it is too small and too centrally planned. The former point was discussed in Chapter 1. The latter, which far exceeds the topic of this book, is the main subject of Barnes and Barr (1988). Given the conflict between the DES and the Treasury a key topic is whether students and universities/polytechnics should have the freedom between them to decide which subjects a given student should study.

The issue of individual choice versus manpower planning was discussed in Chapter 1.2. Arguments of principle suggest that students are able to make sensible choices, and that central planning is likely to be unsuccessful. Practical experience confirms these arguments. From the mid 1970s, the University Grants Committee (UGC) increasingly became a central planning body, and one which has been heavily criticised. Its decisions have been attacked, and so has the way it has reached those decisions. There has been a lack of openness and accountability, giving rise to suspicions, whether justified or not, that some decisions were arbitrary.

In addition, there has been an increasingly burdensome paper chase. The UGC issues at least 40 Circulars to universities annually, usually calling for some kind of response which requires data to be collected. Often the data are those which the institution would in any case collect for its own purposes, but that is far from always the case. Though the costs of unnecessary data collection have not been quantified, it has been estimated that externally-imposed information gathering at one (relatively small) institution takes up the equivalent of one full-time senior administrator.

The process is costly and of highly dubious effectiveness (for analysis of central planning of UK higher education and its defects, see Barnes and Barr (1988, Chs 1,2 and 3)). A current example, albeit anecdotal, illustrates the point. An eminent scientist at a conference in 1988 pointed out that the graduates in greatest demand in Canada were those with degrees in philosophy, since one of the leading edges of information technology is 'fuzzy logic', research on which requires an understanding of the nature of logic. Philosophy departments in Britain are currently under serious threat. Enough said.

## 2.2 Problems with the Grant System

**The grant system** in its present form was introduced in the Education Act 1962 after a government enquiry (UK, 1960).[1] UK students in full-time higher education receive two forms of direct assistance from the tax-funded grant system: tuition fees are paid by the state; and the student receives a maintenance grant. The full grant varies according to where the student studies and whether or not he/she continues to live in the parental home. The 1989/90 full grant is £2650 for students in higher education in London, £2155 for students elsewhere, and £1710 for students living at home.

The maintenance grant is generally means tested on parental income. Students from the best-off families receive no grant at all, though their fees continue to be tax-funded in full. Where students receive less than the full grant, parents are expected to make a parental contribution equal to the difference between the grant actually received and the full grant.

In its early days the system worked well, and the grant was sufficient for its purpose. Over the years, however, public spending constraints in combination with increasing student numbers put the system under increasing pressure. The resulting problems are well-documented (Barr and Low, 1988; Cornish and Windle, 1988) and require only brief summary.

**Student poverty** The real value of the grant has fallen under all governments, so that its purchasing power today is 25 per cent below its 1962 level. As a result, the DES in evidence to the Select Committee on Education and Science in 1986 stated that, 'we would not maintain that the [grant] is sufficient to meet all the essential expenditure of the average student'.

Parallel to this trend has been an increase in the parental contribution from £468 in 1962/3 to £827 in 1987/8 at constant prices.[2] In 1987/8 students on average received 60 per cent of their maintenance from the grant and 40 per cent from contributions (UK, 1988, para. 2.2). The system works badly. About half the students who are entitled to a parental contribution receive less than the assessed amount, and the shortfall is substantial; students whose parents give them less than the grant system supposes receive only £53 of every £100 of assessed parental contribution (Barr and Low, 1988, pp 31–4).

Thus the full grant is too low to support a student fully, and many students do not receive even that amount. As a result, about one student in 13 in 1982/3 remained below the long-term supplementary benefit level even when income from all sources was included (Barr and Low, 1988, Table 6), a picture which has almost certainly worsened in the intervening years.

**Parental wealth** Though many students are poor, their parents, typically, are not. Compared with the population at large, students (averaged across all universities and polytechnics) are twice as likely to come from higher-income families (the top 40 per cent of incomes), and over three times as likely to come from the highest incomes (roughly the top 12½ per cent). Put another way, the parents of students in higher education appear twice as frequently at higher incomes as they would if students were drawn at random from the population as a whole.

At Oxford and Cambridge the disproportion is even greater. Students there are 2½ times as likely to come from higher-income families and nearly four times as likely to come from those with the highest incomes.

Grants overall are therefore redistributive towards the better-off. They offer assistance to young people who proceed to higher education, with no comparable assistance for most individuals in other sorts of education, or those requiring financial backing to invest in physical rather than human capital. The President of the National Union of Students, in a recent article (Sherlock, 1988), defended the grant system as 'an integrated, targeted student finance system'. This is correct. It is targeted with some precision on the middle class. Students tend to come from better-off families, and their subsequent earnings are 25 per cent higher than the earnings of the average taxpayer.[3] To those who follow the literature on such matters (Goodin and Le Grand, 1987) this should come as no surprise.

**Cost of the system** The British taxpayer makes one of the largest contributions per student to maintenance (as distinct from fees) of any country. UK recurrent spending per student on maintenance in 1984 was £750; the Netherlands spent £360 per year, France £180, West Germany £70 and Japan £30 (UK, 1988, Chart 6). This would not be a major problem if only a small system of higher education were needed. The Anderson Committee (UK, 1960) assumed that the grant system would support around 175,000 students; today around 400,000 students receive a mandatory award (UK, 1988, para 2.3). The grant system is thus expensive. It is this fact more than any other which has kept the higher-education sector in Britain small, since the taxpayer cost of expanding the system is high. It is no exaggeration to say that the grant system, far from increasing opportunity, is the single greatest *impediment* to access and expansion;[4] and Chapter 4 argues that the White Paper proposals serve only to aggravate the problem.

## 2.3 Constraints on Expansion within the Current System

**Expanding the grant system,** if taken seriously, would necessitate raising the grant by about 25 per cent to restore its mid-1960s purchasing power, abolishing the parental contribution and increasing by at least 50 per cent the number of grants on offer. Expenditure on the grant in 1987/8 was £829 million. Abolishing the parental contribution (payable for about two-thirds of all students, at an average level of about 40 per cent of the total grant) raises the cost to about £1.35 billion; raising the grant by 25 per cent and the number of grants by 50 per cent raises the total cost to around £2½ billion.

A complete solution via the grant system thus raises costs by over £1½ billion, to which figure must be added the non-maintenance costs of increasing the number of places by 50 per cent. A case can be made for spending an additional £1½ billion on higher education. But to spend it all on grants would be to benefit mainly the middle class and would, in addition, totally violate the strategy in Chapter 1, that there should be a reduction in public spending on maintenance, the savings being used to expand the system and to improve access by helping at the 16–19 level.

**Limitations of parental contributions** Though the system of student support in most countries relies heavily on parents, the suitability of such a mechanism in the run-up to the twenty-first century is open to question. It is easy to see how family contributions to student support grew through a process of historical inertia. In times when education was a matter of family choice, and higher education was in any case a concern mainly of the social elite, reliance on family support was both natural and appropriate. It is far from clear that this argument is valid today, when higher education is much more (a) a mass phenomenon and (b) an economic necessity.

The arguments in favour of parental contributions are, first, that they save public spending and therefore allow a larger higher-education sector for a given public-sector cost. Second, since parental support is means tested either *de facto* or *de jure*, it can be argued that they are equitable.[5] Third, students cannot easily borrow from the private sector because they can offer no security. But parents *can* borrow, and so parental contributions can be thought of as an indirect way of giving students access to private-sector loan funds. Parental contributions, from one viewpoint, are an intergenerational mechanism for trying to deal with a failure in capital markets. The counter-argument is that a good loan system would be a much better way of dealing with this market failure.

There are other strong counter-arguments. First, far from allowing higher education to grow by keeping down public costs, parental contributions can keep the system small since attempts to expand the system by increasing the parental contribution can lead to a revolt amongst middle-class parents (e.g. the 1985 Tory revolt described in Chapter 1.1). Second, parental support in practice can be very patchy: this is certainly the case in the UK. At least two countries (West Germany and Austria) have made parental contributions legally binding precisely to prevent non-payment; in all other countries they remain, in essence, voluntary. If parental contributions are voluntary, their coverage is likely to be uneven, making them inefficient even in their own terms. Making them compulsory solves that problem but turns them, in effect, into a tax on the parents of academically successful children—a somewhat bizarre notion.

The conclusion is that it is neither feasible nor desirable to try to solve the problems of the present system by expanding it. The possibility of expansion is limited by political considerations, by competing claims on tax revenues (especially in the light of demographic prospects) and by the distributionally regressive character of such expansion were it to occur.

# 3 Non-Solution 2: Lessons from Abroad

Since the UK has no experience of student loans it is necessary to seek evidence elsewhere. Section 1 therefore surveys very briefly the principal sources of student support in some other countries. The rest of the chapter analyses the problems which arise from badly-designed loan systems.

## 3.1 Sources of Student Support in Different Countries

This is an area where institutions are complex, change rapidly and are not written up in any easily accessible form. In addition, conversion to a common currency faces familiar problems. Comparisons are therefore only approximate. This chapter relies heavily on international data in the White Paper (UK, 1988, Annex C) and on the writing of Johansson and Ricknell (1985), Johnstone (1986) and Woodhall (1983a and b); for fuller discussion of the material in this section, see Barr (1989). Two sets of data are discussed: public expenditure on student support in different countries; and the contributions to total support by four sets of actors: the student, their parents, the taxpayer and universities/philanthropic institutions.

**Public expenditure on student support** is shown in Figures 1A and 1B (taken from UK, 1988, Annex C, Charts A and B). The following conclusions all relate to public spending on students' living expenses (i.e. they do not relate to tuition fees).[1]

△The maximum support per individual student (Figure 1A) varies widely from country to country. The countries with the highest levels of publicly-funded support include Norway, the Netherlands and the UK; those with the lowest are France, Ireland and Japan. The maximum public spending per student in Norway is over 3½ times what it is in Ireland.

△The proportion of students receiving public-sector support (Figure 1B) also varies widely, from a peak of 90 per cent in the Netherlands and 82 per cent in the UK to a low of 12 per cent in France and Japan.

△The UK's high level of public spending on student support emerges clearly from the previous two points. Of the countries in Figure 1A which have a maximum grant per head of over £2000 per year, only the UK and the Netherlands are also amongst the countries in Figure 1B in which the great majority of students are eligible for at least some tax-funded assistance with living costs.

△ Virtually all countries (the exceptions in Figure 1A are Japan and West Germany) have a grant system of some sort for undergraduates, but the maximum per student varies from over £2000 in Australia, the Netherlands and the UK to a negligible amount in Sweden. Not only does the maximum value of the grant vary; so does its rate of taper as parental income rises. The maximum UK grant is due to fall as loans are phased in; in Sweden the grant element is due to rise.

△ Most countries have a loan system (of the countries in Figure 1A, only France and Ireland neither have one nor have any current plan to introduce one). Again, though, the amount of loan varies widely, from a maximum of £2774 in Norway down to £761 in Denmark.

△ The relative contribution of loan and grant varies widely. In France the grant is small and there is no loan scheme; in Japan, the maximum loan is small and there is no grant.

△ The overall conclusion is that there is nothing systematic in the pattern of public spending on student support in different countries.

**Contributions to student support** are shown in Figures 2A, B and C, taken from Johnstone (1986, pp 148–52). The figures show the contribution to the costs of higher education by four groups: the students themselves via loans, their parents, the taxpayer and universities/philanthropic institutions. The three figures illustrate the shares in total higher-education costs of these four groups for low-, middle- and high-income families. The following are the major elements in the story the figures tell.

△ The taxpayer share is considerable in all countries for low-income families, but declines sharply as family income rises and is negligible at high incomes.

△ The parents' share follows the opposite pattern. It is zero or negligible for low-income families and very substantial for high-income families. Only in Sweden is there little parental contribution even at high incomes. Where the UK stands out, is that parents with high incomes are expected to meet the *whole* cost of student support, though this will change with the introduction of loans.

△ The students' share is through loans. Their relation to income is more complex than the pattern for taxpayers and parents. Indebtedness remains broadly constant for low- and middle-income families, but tends to decline at high incomes: this is partly because loans in most countries are means tested on parental income, and also because students from better-off families receive more help from their parents and therefore need to borrow less. Only Sweden shows no sign of this inverse relationship.

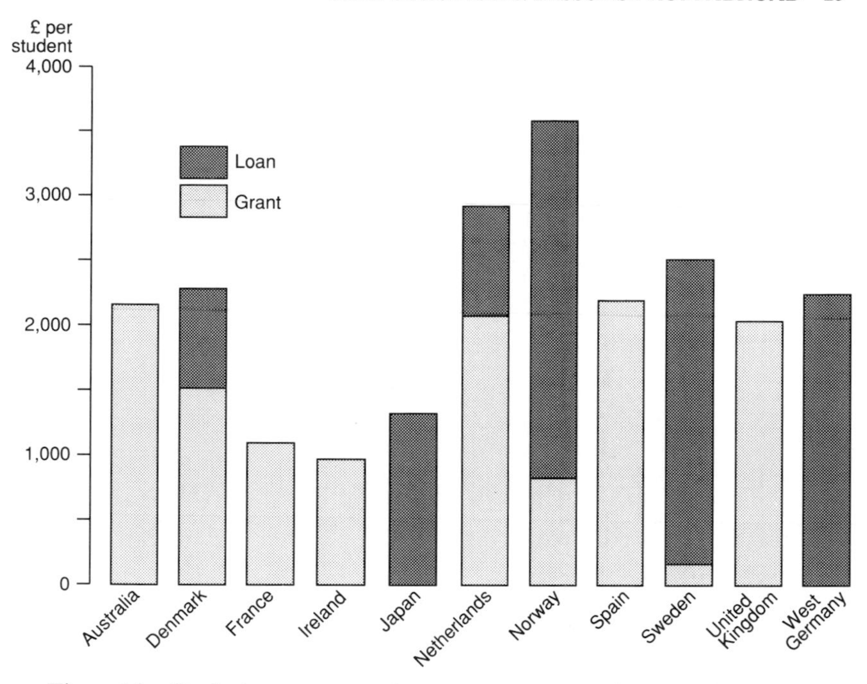


Figure 1A Student support: maximum government assistance, 1987–8

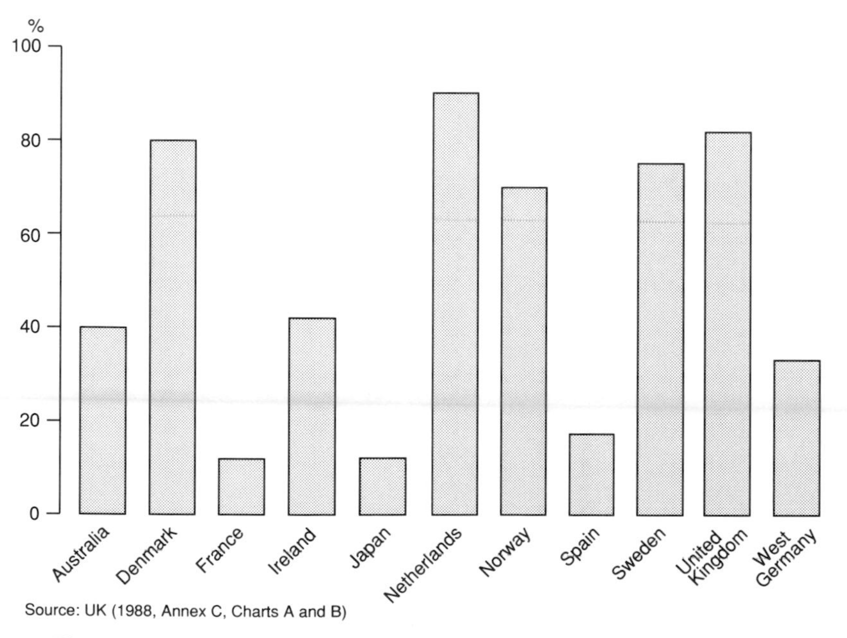


Source: UK (1988, Annex C, Charts A and B)

Figure 1B Proportion of students receiving government assistance

△Only in the USA is the institutional/philanthropic share significant—and that contribution, too, declines as family income rises.

△To paint a very broad-brush picture, at low incomes students are supported mainly by the taxpayer and by loans; at high incomes they are supported mainly by their parents and (to a much smaller extent) by loans.

△Finally, note the absence of any contribution by industry (one of the few countries in which industry makes a non-trivial contribution to student maintenance is Poland). Since industry is one of the main beneficiaries of higher education this conclusion is surprising. The matter is discussed further in Chapter 5.3.

## 3.2 The Problems of Mortgage-Type Loans

The way out of the problems discussed in Chapter 2 is at least partially to switch to loans. However, it is vital to choose the right scheme. It is surprising the extent to which most people (including, alas, most students) still see the issue as a two-way debate between grants and loans. In reality, it is a three-way debate between grants, mortgage-type loans and loans with income-related repayments.

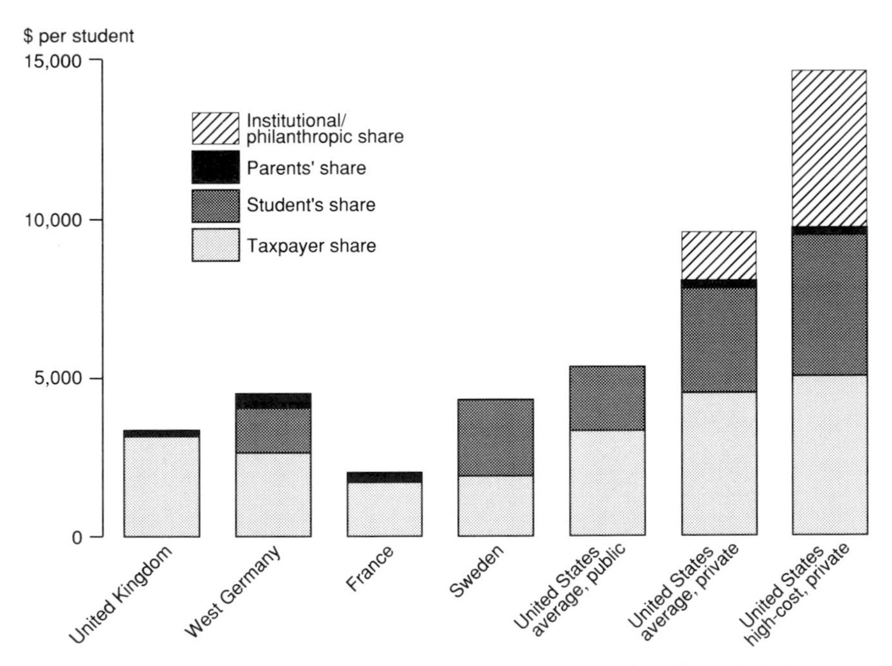


Figure 2A Costs of higher education: low-income families, 1985–6

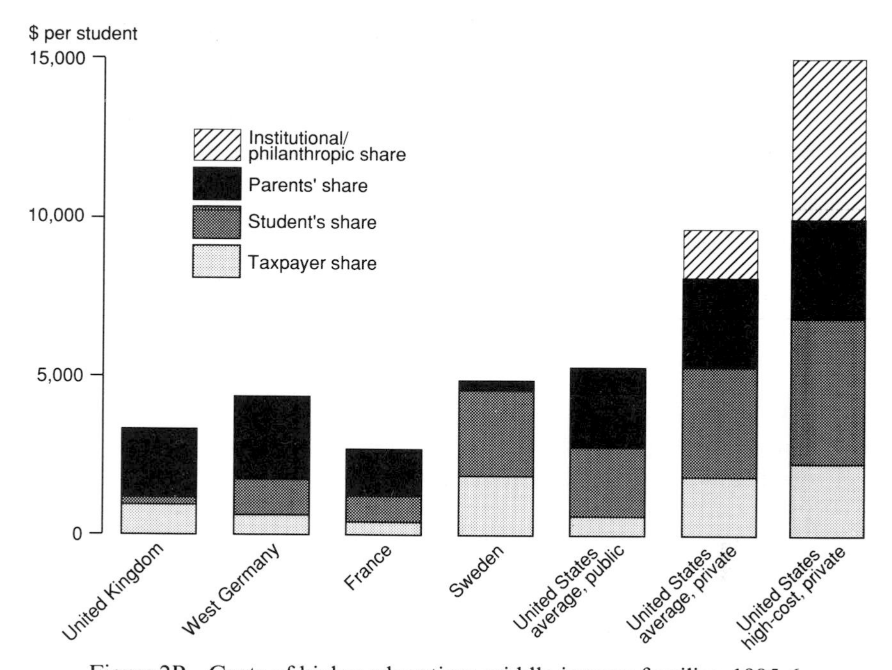


Figure 2B Costs of higher education: middle-income families, 1985–6

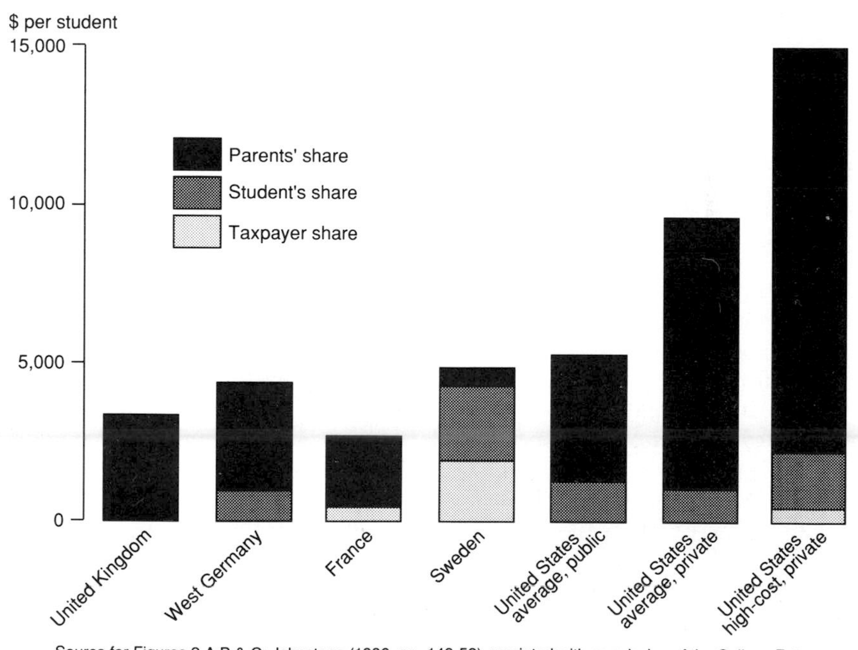


Source for Figures 2 A B & C: Johnstone (1986, pp. 148-52), reprinted with permission of the College Entrance Examination Board, New York, copyright 1986

Figure 2C Costs of higher education: high-income families, 1985–6

This section argues that reliance on the mortgage model as the primary source of undergraduate loans would be catastrophic. Mortgage loans reduce access on the demand side by discouraging applicants and *de facto* preventing parental contributions being abolished; on the supply side, they rule out expansion because they are expensive in public spending terms and involve high administrative costs; and they have a variety of deleterious incentive effects. The specifics of mortgage loans in the framework of the White Paper are discussed in Chapter 4.

**Reduced access on the demand side** Mortgage-type loans are risky from the individual student's point of view, and so deter applicants, most particularly those from disadvantaged backgrounds. Middle-class students might take them up; but the whole point of loans in to enable *new* students to enter the system. Many marginal students will be deterred. The result is wasted talent and reduced intergenerational mobility.

It is sometimes argued (UK, 1988, Chart J) that people from the lower socioeconomic groups will take out a mortgage to buy a house, so why would they not borrow to buy a degree? It is important to nail this myth. Leaving aside the tax advantages for house purchase, when someone buys a house (a) he knows what he is buying (since he has lived in a house all his life), (b) the house is unlikely to fall down, and (c) the value of the house is likely to go up. In contrast, people who borrow to pay for a degree, (a) are not fully certain what they are buying (particularly if they come from a family with no graduates), (b) there is a high risk (or at least a high perceived risk) of failing the degree outright, and (c) not all degrees carry a high rate of return—graduates can be unemployed, and fashions and job prospects can change.

For all three reasons, borrowing to buy a degree is considerably more risky to the individual than borrowing to buy a house, and the risks are likely to be greater for people from poorer backgrounds and for women. The rates of return in the White Paper (UK, 1988, Annex D), it should be noted, are averages across all undergraduates; what is being discussed here is not the average outcome, but the variance.

A separate way in which mortgage-type loans can hinder access is through parental contributions. At least some parents discourage their offspring from going into higher education out of a reluctance to pay parental contributions; the same effect *mutatis mutandis* discourages at least some students from applying. Mortgage-type loans let neither parents nor students off the hook. Irrespective of the formal situation, many parents would feel under moral pressure to prevent their offspring going too deeply into mortgage-type debt. Whether or not parental contributions continue formally, they are likely to discourage applications at the margin.

**Reduced access on the supply side** arises because long-term student loans are also risky to the lender. Mortgage-type loans have a high public-sector cost and, in consequence, do not readily enable the system to expand; they also are inflexible and administratively costly.

There is a myth that pure private-sector mortgage loans from commercial banks would instantly put more money into students' pockets without the need for any increase in public spending. This is false, and would remain false even if the Treasury rules about government guarantees were suspended.[2]

The fact of the matter is that private financial markets for long-run student loans do not work very well (if they did, such loans would already be on offer). The main reason is the riskiness to the lender because there is no collateral (contrast the case of lending for house purchase). If the legalisation of slavery is ruled out, the private sector will make long-term unsecured loans only with a Treasury guarantee. And the Treasury guarantee is not just a bit of paper—it will be costly. The USA is an example of the resulting problems, in particular high default rates.[3] If repayments are collected by the commercial banks, the White Paper assumption that 25 per cent of loans will never be repaid because of default and write-off is, if anything, on the conservative side. Chapter 4 explores these matters in detail.

Because the Treasury guarantee is expensive, the resulting system cannot easily be expanded. Both total lending and the type of student eligible will be strictly policed; and there will be a battle between the DES and the Treasury every time it is proposed to raise the ceiling on the amount a student can borrow or to offer loans to new classes of student. Note that the least risky students are those already in higher education, and that those whom expansion is meant to embrace are likely, on average, to be somewhat higher risk. The scheme, in short, offers very little scope for expanding the *number* of students in higher education.

It is sometimes argued that state institutions like the grant system are inflexible (true), and that private-sector institutions are likely to be more flexible. This is another myth: the Treasury guarantee makes it inevitable that student borrowers would have to conform with stringent Treasury-ordained criteria to qualify for a loan. Mortgage-type loans thus do little to expand the *types* of student in higher education.

In addition to the costs of the Treasury guarantee, there would also be high administrative costs. Banks would need to keep a detailed record of each borrower. More important, the cost of chasing up payments would be substantial, the more so because the loan is unsecured (repayments in respect of house purchase can be enforced by the threat of foreclosure; there is no analogue in this case). The Swedish government's Study Assistance Committee, reporting in 1987, concluded that the administrative costs of their (private sector) loan scheme were so high it would have been cheaper simply to give the students the money.

At first sight these costs fall on the private sector. But commercial banks will be reluctant to administer student loans unless they receive at least partial recompense, which returns much of the cost to the public sector. Further public-sector costs will arise each time the Treasury loan guarantee is called into play.

Administrative costs will be heaviest for the more risky students so, again, financial pressures will militate against expansion of the types of student going into higher education.

**Adverse incentives** arise in respect of labour supply, the choice of subject and career, and over inter-temporal decisions. The White Paper (UK, 1988, para 3.15, Option A) suggests that repayments might be suspended where earnings fall below 85 per cent of the national average. The likely labour supply disincentives caused by such 'spikes', as well as the high cost of administration, are discussed in Chapter 4.

Mortgage-type loans will also influence at the margin the student's choice of subject and career. A student who has taken out a large loan will seek to earn enough to repay in comfort. The resulting incentive is to take a vocational degree and to seek a high paying job. The Treasury view is that mortgage-type repayments are to be encouraged precisely because they make the student starkly aware of the costs of his/her decisions. Such a policy is efficient only if one believes that wages always reflect fully the marginal social product of the job, and that education has no external benefits.

There are at least two counter-arguments. First, mortgage-type loans would discourage education as a consumption good, and would at least partly sacrifice its external benefits. Second, as discussed earlier, doing a degree is much more risky than buying a house, so that there is an efficiency argument for a mechanism which does not face the individual with the entire risk of his/her decision.

A further aspect is the efficiency of intertemporal decisions. Because the individual student bears most of the risk of mortgage-type loans, he/she is likely to minimise the amount of borrowing. Though the evidence on the point is only anecdotal, there is more than a suspicion that students in such circumstances borrow less than is efficient and take on a larger than efficient amount of paid work, with deleterious effects on the quality of their degree. A similar problem is already clearly visible for students with large unpaid parental contributions.

## 3.3 Problems with Subsidised Loans

It is important to be clear about the huge deficiencies of mortgage-type repayments because they are included as one of the options in the White Paper. The great majority of loan systems abroad avoid these problems by relating repayments to the individual student's subsequent income (the two main exceptions are the USA and Finland). But loan systems elsewhere fail to avoid two further pitfalls: excessive reliance on subsidised loans; and organising both loan and repayment in nominal terms.

**Subsidised loans** Virtually all loan systems are subsidised, mostly heavily; the result is a mixture of pure loan and implicit grant. Though the intuitive appeal of such a policy is understandable, intuition in this case should be resisted. The resulting system is inefficient and inequitable.

It is inequitable because students tend to come from better-off families and so the subsidy is distributionally regressive. In equity terms it makes much more sense to charge a market interest rate, and channel the saved interest subsidy into a redistributive grant.

Interest subsidies are inefficient, first, if the interest rate has any bearing on a student's decision as to the balance between supporting him/herself by current earnings or, through a loan, out of future earnings. Second, the interest subsidy gives students an incentive to borrow an inefficiently large amount and invest the proceeds in privatisation flotations. There is a counter-argument. If some students (particularly those from poorer backgrounds) over-estimate the degree of risk, there might be an efficiency case for a subsidy (see Gordon, 1981; Williams and Gordon, 1981). Again, however, such students might more effectively be encouraged into higher education by giving them a larger grant.

Even without the incentive to excessive borrowing, subsidised loans are expensive, creating pressures to ration the amount each student can borrow. In West Germany, for instance, loans are means tested on the income of parents and of the student him/herself, with the result that only about one third of students are eligible. A similar phenomenon arises in other countries. In addition to pressures to ration the amount each student can borrow, high costs can also act to keep the system small; such pressures will come from the Treasury if the subsidy is tax-funded, and from the banks if they underwrite part of the cost.

Interest subsidies are thus inefficient if they distort intertemporal choices; and they create inequity through their distributional impact, and *a fortiori* if their cost keeps the system small and hence excludes potential students from entering higher education. In contrast, if banks receive around the market rate of interest and repayment is reliable, they will be happy to expand the scheme to meet student demand, just as over the years lending for house purchase has risen without the need for any negotiation or heavy political pleading by home buyers. Market interest rates, in short, can make a useful contribution to the expansion of higher education.

**Indexation** There is a strong argument for loans to be indexed to some sensible measure of the rate of inflation, both for efficiency and to prevent the arbitrary redistributive effects of inflation. If the loan idea is taken seriously then, in steady state (i.e. with constant population size, etc.), the repayments of one generation of students should be sufficient to make identical loans to a later generation. If loans are indexed, this is exactly what happens. If they are not and nominal interest rates fail to keep pace with inflation, the loan system will redistribute from future generations of students and/or taxpayers to the present generation of students. Such redistribution is arbitrary; it is also a form of implied subsidy. Both features are inequitable; the latter, for the reasons discussed above, is also inefficient.

## 3.4 Lessons from Home and Abroad

The arguments of Chapters 2 and 3 can be summarised as a series of principles which should inform any system of student support.

**Principle 1** Given the external benefits it creates, higher education should receive substantial taxpayer support. But there are also major private benefits, and so the individual student should meet at least part of the costs of his/her maintenance.

**Principle 2** For the reasons set out in Chapter 2.3, there should be a shift in the emphasis of support from the family to the individual student. It is both inefficient and inequitable that students should be *compelled* to depend on their parents. Even judged in its own terms, the system of parental contributions does not work well. Any reformed system of student support should reduce such dependency by giving students access to their future earnings.

**Principle 3** Since doing a degree is risky (Chapter 3.2), student support mechanisms, for both efficiency and equity reasons, should offer protection against individual risk.

Principle 1 implies a partial shift away from grants; Principle 2 implies a shift away from heavy reliance on parental contributions. The two together point towards loans, but Principle 3 implies that loans should not leave the individual student carrying all the risk. Hence:

**Principle 4** Loans should have repayments related to the subsequent income of the individual student.

**Principle 5** There are strong arguments for the retention of some grants. Their main function, however, should not be general support, but to bring about a level playing field between different groups of students.

Two sorts of student stand out: those facing higher costs, and those coming from poorer backgrounds. Mature students are an example of the former (family responsibilities, mortgages, etc.) and should receive a larger grant if it is wished to encourage them to enter higher education. Similarly, there could be a larger grant for London students (who face higher-than-average housing costs) if it is thought appropriate that students should face similar costs wherever they study. There might also be some equalisation for students doing longer-than-average degrees, e.g. those studying languages or (possibly) medicine, or those studying at a Scottish university. There should certainly be a larger grant on equity grounds for poorer students. There is also an efficiency argument for doing so if students from disadvantaged backgrounds over-estimate the risk involved in doing a degree.

**Principle 6** For reasons of efficiency and equity, loans should be substantially unsubsidised and should be indexed to the rate of inflation. Loans are a device for giving students access to their future earnings. Distributional goals should be achieved through the application of Principle 5.

**Principle 7** Since employers are one of the main beneficiaries, a mechanism should be found whereby industry can contribute to the cost of higher education.

A final conclusion follows from these principles: that systems of student support should be designed as a coherent *strategy*, not as a patchwork of *ad hoc* policies. If grants and parental support are to be partly replaced by loans with income-related repayments, the loan scheme should not itself cause inefficiency or inequity by being a muddled (and often expensive) mixture of loan and implicit grant.

Chapter 4 shows how the White Paper scheme fails to meet several of these principles; the scheme proposed in Chapter 5 is designed, to the maximum extent possible, to conform with all of them.

# 4 Non-Solution 3: The White Paper

## 4.1 Introductory Matters

The White Paper (UK, 1988) was late in arriving, and lacking any coherent strategy when it did. As explained in Chapter 1.4, this was not the fault of its writers: it was doomed from the start because the objectives it was written to meet were wholly incompatible.[1]

**Outline of the White Paper scheme and the proposed alternative** Though many aspects of the White Paper scheme were left open at the time of publication, the outline proposal was the following. Students would be able to borrow up to £420 in the first year. The source of the funds would be the Treasury, but both the loan and repayments would be administered by the banking system. No interest is charged, but the loan is indexed to the rate of inflation (i.e. if prices double, the student repays twice the nominal amount he/she borrowed). The grant would be frozen, and as prices rose the loan element would rise until students were supported 50 per cent by the grant and parental contribution and 50 per cent by the loan. The parental contribution, in consequence, is frozen but not abolished. In terms of today's prices, once the scheme is fully phased in, students in London would receive £1325 (half of the 1989/90 London grant) in grant/parental contribution and borrow up to £1325 in addition. The key element left undecided is how repayments should be arranged.

It is useful to anticipate briefly the alternative scheme proposed in Chapter 5. Students do not borrow Treasury funds and repay via the banks (the White Paper proposal), but borrow from the banks and repay in the form of a small addition to graduates' National Insurance Contributions (NICs). The arithmetic in Chapter 5.2 suggests that it would be possible to repay an indexed loan equal to half the London grant at a 2 per cent interest rate over 25 years for an addition of $1\frac{1}{4}$p to the NICs of graduates, i.e. instead of paying nine pence in the pound which most people currently pay, graduates would pay $10\frac{1}{4}$p.

The rest of this section discusses some of the (relatively speaking) minor problems with the White Paper, before proceeding to its strategic problems. Section 2 analyses the incentive effects of the mortgage model; section 3 outlines the major problems caused by reliance on the banking sector to collect repayments, and section 4, which is slightly technical, discusses in some detail the use of Treasury funds as the source of student borrowing and the Ryrie rules, which specify how Treasury guarantees should be accounted for in public expenditure. This sets the scene for section 5 which discusses the true costs of the White Paper proposals and the savings offered by the National Insurance scheme. The costs of the White Paper scheme (in absolute terms and relative to the National Insurance scheme, and however they are measured) are gigantic and wholly rule out any expansion in either the short or the long run.

**The withdrawal of social security benefits** The White Paper proposes that students (other than those who are disabled, or single parents) will no longer be eligible for income support, unemployment benefit or housing benefit, and 80 per cent of the cost saving set out in Annex E of the White Paper derives from the withdrawal of those benefits.

The first question is the effect on students' incomes. The government claims that the average benefit receipt of those students who received any benefit at all in 1986/7 was £249. Since the loan offered in the White Paper is £420, it is argued that the average student will be better off even allowing for the loss of benefit. Though true for the typical student receiving benefit, it is necessary to consider also the variance in benefit receipts. If the average benefit is £249, a non-trivial number of students must be receiving more than £420, and the income of such students is unambiguously reduced, and for the minority with substantial benefit receipts reduced substantially. London students with high housing costs figure prominently in the latter group.

The deeper question is whether it is appropriate to remove students' entitlement to benefit. It can be argued that benefits designed to support the very poor are different in character from those providing support for students, whose income is low only as a temporary life-cycle effect, and that the system of student support should obviate the need for poverty relief. There is much merit in that argument, and I would accept it but for the empirical fact that housing costs vary enormously on an individual basis which can adequately be captured only by a mechanism which takes account of the situation of individual students. Thus there is a strong case for allowing students continued eligibility for housing benefit. There is no similar case for the other benefits.

**Other issues** Two are worth mentioning. First, the White Paper claims that its loan scheme will increase students' incomes. This claim, we have seen, is false for the sizeable minority of students receiving more than £420 per year in social security benefits. In addition, the £420 borrowed under the White Paper scheme counts towards a student's total indebtedness when applying for a conventional bank overdraft (a fact which has been confirmed by the banking sector). To that extent, for those students who already have debts of £420 or more, the White Paper scheme increases their income only to the extent that the student loan has a lower interest rate than the overdraft. It does not otherwise add to the student's income at all, in contrast with the National Insurance scheme, borrowing from which will not be included by banks in a student's total indebtedness (this fact, too, has been checked). In short, for many students the White Paper scheme will do little to increase their income; and it can be argued that those whom it fails to help are disproportionately those who most need additional assistance.

A further point is the effect of the freezing of the grant until students are supported 50 per cent by the grant/parental contribution and 50 per cent by the loan. Under the present system, mature students and those studying in London receive a higher grant in recognition of their higher costs. The move to the 50:50 ratio has the effect of halving the mature student and London differentials; even more important, it similarly erodes the differential for students from disadvantaged backgrounds. If the differential under present arrangements is appropriate, such erosion violates Principle 5 (Chapter 3.4).

## 4.2 The Mortgage Model and Incentive Effects

The White Paper suggests that students borrow from Treasury funds, the loans being disbursed by the banks, and repayments collected by the banking system. Repayment models include mortgage-type loans (the main example being Option A) and loans with income-related repayments (Option D). This section discusses the White Paper proposals mainly in terms of Option A. Section 5 sets out a specific version of Option D.

Under Option A (para 3.15) loans are repaid rather like an indexed mortgage, save that repayment is suspended where earnings are low (I shall stick to the White Paper's example of 85 per cent of national average income). Suppose the student's repayment was £400 per year. The 85 per cent threshold, taken at face value, means that a small increase in earnings could take a graduate across the threshold, bringing a liability for a large repayment. This 'spike' would be an additional manifestation of the poverty trap, one of whose main effects is to give people no incentive to increase their earnings unless they can increase them substantially.

The White Paper acknowledges this by talking of 'a tapering scale of repayments' where income is only a little above the threshold, thus breaking down the big 'spike' into several smaller ones. This reduces the intensity of the disincentive, but at the price of having a disincentive over a wider range of earnings.

The effect of such 'spikes' is predictable. There will be an incentive for (particularly) women to work part-time, at least until the age of 50 (the age at which any unpaid loan is written off). Such an incentive would be particularly unfortunate at a time when demographic pressures require maximum labour force participation, especially on the part of the most highly skilled people.

## 4.3 Collection of Repayments via the Banking Sector

Loans with income-related repayments (Option D) are desirable on educational grounds. But they are ruled out by their vast administrative cost if repayments are collected by banks, which would have to duplicate many of the functions of the Inland Revenue. The use of banks as the collection mechanism requires the choice of Options A, B or C (i.e. mortgage-type repayments), because those are the only ones which banks could administer.

However, the costs of administering even Option A, which at first sight appears very simple, are far higher than is immediately apparent; and the costs of Options B and C would be even greater. It is necessary to discuss how repayment for low-income graduates would be suspended, the size of the losses through default and write-off, and the time flow of repayments.

**Administering the suspension of repayment** Option A's 85 per cent trigger, below which repayment is suspended, is, in effect, a complex, cumbersome, obtrusive means test applied by banks. The trigger could work only if employed graduates sent their P60 to their bank manager to establish entitlement to suspension;[2] unemployed graduates could submit their UB40; for the non-employed (e.g. women working in the home bringing up children) no mechanism exists at all. Any such regime faces two strategic problems: from the viewpoint of resource allocation it is administratively complex and hence costly (reaffirming Lord Robbins' assertion in the quote in Chapter 1.3); and from the viewpoint of individual banks it creates major problems for customer relations.

Given the 85 per cent trigger, the only way in which banks could collect repayments is in arrears, with all the consequent disadvantages. A graduate with high earnings in the tax year ending April 1994 would be required to repay in arrears over the tax year ending April 1995. But he/she might have no earnings (or only low earnings) in the second year, e.g. a RADA graduate.[3] Numerically much more important, the problem would arise every time a woman left the labour force to have a baby. This would reintroduce the 'negative dowry' problem in another form, and the necessary avoiding measures would further complicate administration.

An additional problem is the definition of income to be used. If the definition were that on the P60, repayment could bite graduates in receipt of taxable social security benefits, e.g. the receipt of Family Credit could take a large family across the 85 per cent threshold (*Hansard*, 1 December 1988, cols 393–4). Whatever the argument in economic terms, this outcome would hardly be politically appealing.

Alternatively, all (or some) cash benefits could be excluded from the relevant definition of income. In that case banks could not use P60s as evidence of income. What then could they use? Whatever the answer, the result would be yet further administrative costs. Note, too, that when a bank loan is taken out currently, the detailed income checks are made only at the time the loan is taken out; here we are talking about an income check *every year*.

A third issue is who grants the exemption from repayment if income falls below 85 per cent? The tax authorities could issue an exemption certificate for the graduate to present to his/her bank manager. Such a solution, however, is costly and unlikely to commend itself to the Inland Revenue. Alternatively, bank managers could make the decisions. This would impose administrative costs on banks, who might not wish to make such decisions (see the discussion below); and people outside the banking sector might not regard them as the best institutions to make educational decisions. The procedure would also lead to all sorts of local anomalies.

All that remains is the possibility that bank managers operate within a framework of rules established by the DES and/or the Treasury. This would be administratively cumbersome and would lose much of the flexibility claimed for the private sector.

The result is an administrative system of considerable complexity and huge cost. It is well known that the Inland Revenue faces a large administrative burden in issuing a P45 and related activity when someone changes job,[4] a phenomenon which occurs with particular frequency in a graduate's early years in the labour force. Such costs apply equally to banks, who would have to bear extra administrative costs precisely at the time when many graduates would not be making any repayments (contrast the case with National Insurance Contributions where the *extra* costs of collection are virtually zero).

A plausible estimate of administrative costs is £100 per student per year, an estimate with which the banks broadly concur (see for instance 'Finance Snag for Student Loans', *Yorkshire Post,* 20 March 1989, p 7). The cost of graduates in high-paid jobs who pay monthly or annually by standing order would be lower; but those of any graduate who had to prove that his/her income was below the 85 per cent threshold would be higher. This adds up to a total of around £50 million per year merely for those students currently in higher education. To them must be added future cohorts, so that total administrative costs (discussed in section 5) are likely to eat up the entire long-run savings of the scheme.

**The size of leakages** A different and equally important issue is the proportion of repayments banks will actually be able to collect. Leakages arise in two forms. First, there are defaults, i.e. fraudulent non-repayment. The White Paper allows for a 10 per cent default rate, which is not implausible, given US experience, where repayments are collected by banks (see Chapter 3, note 3). The White Paper allows *in addition* for a 15 per cent rate of write-off, e.g. where graduates are below the 85 per cent threshold for so long that they never fully repay the loan. Thus, the White Paper accepts that some 25 per cent of lending will leak away, or £131 million per year once the scheme is fully phased in.

Where repayments are collected by banks there is a large leakage. It is important to be very clear about the incentives they face. If banks collect Treasury money, they have no incentive to pursue repayments at all. If they have to bear themselves any losses in excess of the estimated 25 per cent leakage, then they have no incentive to do any further chasing once they have collected 75 per cent of total lending. Thus the guarantee becomes a self-fulfilling prophecy and the maximum leakage becomes the norm.

The government is well aware of the incentive issue. A confidential Conservative Research Department Brief, prepared to 'sell' the White Paper to Conservative backbenchers, denies that the White Paper scheme will experience US-type default rates of 10 per cent or more.

> The relatively high levels of default in America arise partly because there are no general provisions for graduates to defer repayments . . . when income is low; and partly because the banks have found it relatively easy to declare a default and seek a refund from the Government. *These will not be features of the Government's proposed system* (my emphasis).

The quote, taken literally, says that banks will have to face the cost of defaults. There are two responses: (a) banks would not, except under the most intense duress, agree to such a scheme; (b) if the cost of defaults is to fall on the banks, why does the White Paper include over £50 million per year for defaults in the public-sector costs of the scheme in later years?

Leakages are likely to be sharply lower with repayment collected by employers via the National Insurance system. The default rate for NICs is tiny in comparison with the White Paper's 10 per cent. It derives, first, from employers who go bankrupt, the effect of which is minute. Second, is evasion of the black-economy variety. For graduates this will not be a major problem at the low-income end of the spectrum (graduates are not typically part of the 'lump');[5] and at high incomes there is no problem in this context since, even in principle, no NICs are lost above the upper earnings limit.[6] Additionally, whilst the incentive to evade income tax is obvious, there is little incentive to evade NICs, since one's future benefits are involved. A 2 per cent default rate is therefore erring on the side of caution.

Write-offs raise different issues. It is not clear where the 15 per cent White Paper figure comes from, since the size of write-offs depends crucially on the repayment method. If repayments are collected by employers as part of NICs, write-offs will be lower for several reasons.

△ Only graduates who do not earn 20 per cent of average earnings in any single *week* throughout their entire working life will repay nothing at all; given demographic trends such individuals will be increasingly rare. Under Option A, in contrast, a graduate has to exceed 85 per cent over a whole *year* to make any repayment.

△ NI repayments do not contain the major adverse incentives of the very sharp 85 per cent 'spike'. In addition, they are likely to come in earlier and probably also in larger amounts.

△ Given the difficulty of evading NICs it is possible to allow repayments over a longer period. In particular there is no reason whatever to write off loans at age 50, which is just around the time that many married woman graduates (with children off their hands) are likely to return, highly productively, to the labour force.

A third form of leakage, emigration, is discussed in Chapter 5.4.

A plausible estimate of write-offs if repayments are collected as part of the NI mechanism is about half the White Paper rate. Thus total leakages, including a 2 per cent allowance for default, are 10 per cent which is the figure used hereafter.

**The time flow of repayments** is also affected by whether they are collected by banks. Three factors have a crucial influence: the repayment method used; the time path of graduate earnings; and the extent of the disincentive created by the 85 per cent 'spike'. It is not clear on what basis the loan repayments in Annex E of the White Paper were calculated.

Under Option A, repayment starts at 85 per cent of average earnings at which point (apart from any tapering) repayments are made in full. With NICs, repayment starts at the lower earnings limit[7] (around 20 per cent of average earnings), with repayment made only in part.

Thus with Option A repayments tend to come later and larger; with Option D they will at first be smaller, but they will come sooner, probably much sooner. The timing of repayments depends not only on the repayment method, but also on the time path of graduate earnings. Since these are not known in any detail, the following observations, of necessity, are somewhat *a priori.*

△With Option A (to exaggerate) there will be no one at 86 per cent of average earnings, but lots of people at 84 per cent. This tendency will delay repayments.

△One of the many virtues of indexed repayments is that only a low interest rate is necessary, since inflation is dealt with by inflating the principal and making repayments out of higher earnings in the future (see Appendix 2). With the 2 per cent interest rate suggested in Chapter 5, the additional NICs on a loan equal to half the grant will fully repay the interest component for someone earning around half the national average. Thus even at a relatively unsubsidised interest rate, increases in indebtedness can be avoided for all but the poorest graduates. This serves to speed up repayment.

△NICs bring in repayments significantly earlier and in larger amounts than does income tax in Option D. Repayments in the latter case start at the income tax threshold. With NICs (a) they start at the lower earnings limit, which is considerably smaller than the income tax threshold, (b) unlike income tax, there is no tax-free allowance, and (c) the NIC threshold is based on weekly rather than annual income. For all three reasons, more repayments come in at lower incomes under NICs than under income tax, and *a fortiori* more than under Option A.

The conclusion is that the time flow of repayments is likely to be more favourable, and possibly (depending on the strength of the disincentive effect of Option A) considerably more favourable in the National Insurance case.

**The view from the banking sector** is dismal. There are two strategic problems. First, there are substantial administrative costs and leakages, and an unfavourable time path of repayments. This problem is soluble so far as banks are concerned (though not in terms of rational resource allocation) if all such costs are met by the taxpayer.

The other strategic problem is the way Option A puts at risk long-term relations with the banks' best prospective customers. Pouring large sums of government money on banks does nothing whatever to address this issue. Banks do not wish to jeopardise relations by acting, in some respects, as the government's debt collector where repayment is laggard. As one bank spokesman put it, '[banks] would have little to gain, and might actually lose student customers, by becoming debt-collectors on behalf of the government' (Johnson, 1989).

Second, many graduates would resent having to submit their P60 to the bank manager. Students are bright, and respond to prevailing incentives: a typical solution would be that a student, having taken out a loan with Barclays, would after graduation submit his P60 as required, but would ensure privacy by transferring his account to the Midland. Most bank employees for similar reasons have their account at another bank. Option A thus systematically drives a wedge between banks and graduates. It follows that banks will be reluctant to administer a means test via the P60, and any other form of income test would be even worse. As someone in the banking sector put it, 'Banks are in business for many and diverse purposes—but means testing is not one of them.'

A third aspect of customer relations is the effect on the bank's image the first time it prosecuted an ex-student for non-paymnent. An LSE student would take out a loan with the NatWest branch next door to the School; if he/she were a popular figure prosecuted relatively soon after graduating the situation is fraught with adverse publicity so far as the bank is concerned.

The view from the banking sector, in short, is that banks are being asked to bear heavy administrative costs, to face large leakages and slow repayments, to offer loans at a zero (i.e. subsidised) real interest rate and to risk systematically losing their best customers. Though discussions with the government were kept quiet, it is known that the reaction of the banks' negotiating team, having confirmed that this was indeed the proposal, was to burst out laughing. As discussed in section 5, the total cost of defaults, administration and the interest subsidy in the White Paper scheme, once it is fully in place, exceeds £450 million *per year*. Laughter seems to be the only response.

The Secretary General of the Committee of London and Scottish Bankers, speaking on BBC Radio 4's *Today* programme on 14 January 1989 confirmed the tenor of discussions rather more circumspectly.

> The banks are . . . worried about who is going to be responsible for determining that a borrower is eligible to have his repayments deferred because his income level is below that percentage prescribed by the government of the national average. And . . . the banks are most concerned about who is going to pick up the bill for any bad debts which inevitably arise in a scheme of this nature . . . It simply is not workable.

## 4.4 The Use of Treasury Funds and the Ryrie Rules

**The use of private funds** The fact that students borrow Treasury money has already been questioned. If the government is serious about a partnership between the public and private sectors, it makes sense to derive the start-up funds for the loan scheme from the private sector, giving rise to an immediate public-expenditure saving which can be used for expansion. The strategy, therefore, is for students to borrow private funds. But banks, for the reasons set out in Chapter 3.2, will not lend to students without some sort of guarantee. At this point the Ryrie rules enter the argument, whereby loans guaranteed by the Treasury count as part of public expenditure. The public-sector cost of student loans thus depends crucially on how the rules are interpreted, a matter of somewhat arcane complexity. The central issue is whether the *whole* of outstanding loans should count as public expenditure or only *that fraction of outstanding loans which the Treasury has agreed to guarantee.*

The starting point is the White Paper calculations of the costs of the loan scheme, which are predicated on a 100 per cent Treasury guarantee to banks and a 25 per cent rate of leakage. Those figures are taken at face value in this section, which shows how the White Paper costs can be sharply reduced by collecting repayments through the National Insurance mechanism and applying the Ryrie rules in a sensible way. Three cases require discussion: those of a 100 per cent Treasury guarantee, a fractional guarantee, and no guarantee.

**Public spending with a 100 per cent guarantee** In this case, total outstanding loans are added to public spending. Additional loans add to the total, repayments reduce it. Thus (UK, 1988, Annex E, reproduced in Table A1, lines 4 and 5) gross lending in the White Paper scheme is £167 million in 1990 and £193 million in 1991; repayments are zero in 1990 and £2 million in 1991. Under strict Ryrie rules the addition to public spending is £167 million in 1990 and £358 million (£167m+£193m–£2m) in 1991. The White Paper calculates the effect of the loan scheme on the Public Sector Borrowing Requirement (PSBR) this way, as shown in Table A1, line 6, illustrated by Figure 3. This is Case 1, that of a 100 per cent guarantee and a 25 per cent leakage: the public-sector cost of the scheme is around £100 million in the early years, with an eventual steady-state saving of about £230 million per year. In the long run, the scheme thus claims to save slightly over one quarter of what is currently spent on student maintenance.

Once the scheme is mature, gross new lending in a particular year is in principle fully offset by repayments, so that there is no increase in outstanding loans, and hence no increase in public spending under Ryrie rules. In practice repayments are less than gross loans because of leakages (default and write-off). Nevertheless, the maximum increase in outstanding loans in any one year is the expected default plus write-off on new lending. The cost of the scheme thus depends crucially on the extent of leakages.

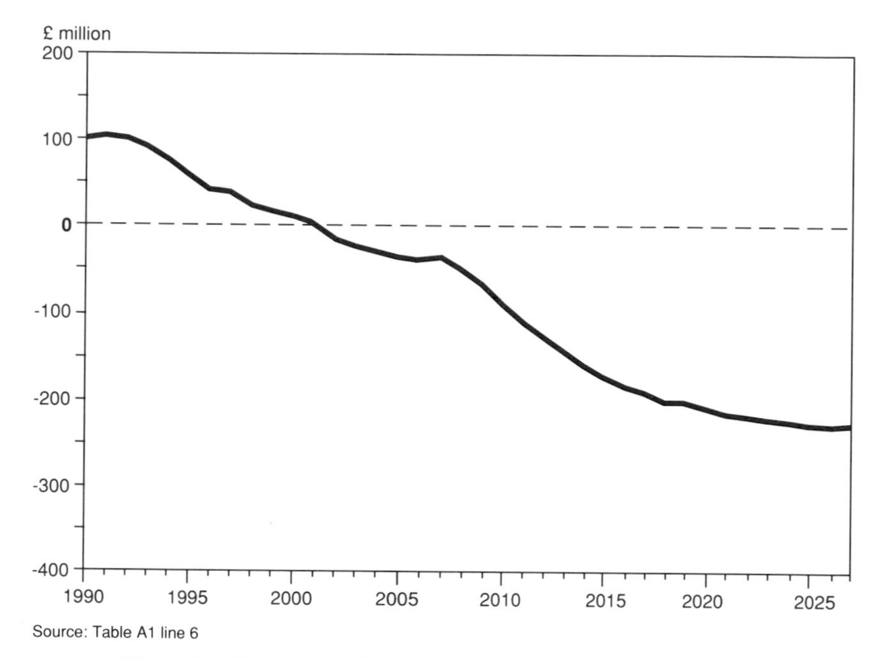


Figure 3 Claimed public expenditure effect of the White Paper

Since the NI scheme, for the reasons discussed in section 3, has smaller leakages, its savings will be larger even with a 100 per cent guarantee. This is Case 2, which assumes a 100 per cent guarantee and a 10 per cent leakage, as shown in lines 9–11 in Table A1 and illustrated by Figure 4. The figures are calculated by inflating line 5 in Table A1 by a factor of 90/75 to reflect the fact that leakages have been reduced from 25 per cent to 10 per cent. Costs in the early years are very similar to Case 1. As Figure 4 shows, however, there are considerable savings in the long run, so that the scheme eventually reduces public spending by around £300 million per year.

**Public spending with a fractional guarantee** Since NI-based repayments have small, predictable leakages, banks could supply the loan funds themselves and would not require a guarantee for more than a percentage of total outstanding debt. If the maximum leakage were 10 per cent, banks could be persuaded to accept a guarantee of (say) 12 per cent. Thus if actual repayments were £900 in respect of £1000 of outstanding loans, banks would be paid the missing £100 out of public funds; but if repayments were £850, banks would be paid only £120 of the missing £150, and would bear the remaining £30 loss themselves.

If banks accepted a guarantee of 12 per cent, the maximum Treasury liability would be 12 per cent of outstanding debt, and so the maximum effect on public spending, even under the strictest interpretation of Ryrie rules, is 12 per cent of outstanding debt. Because repayments based on

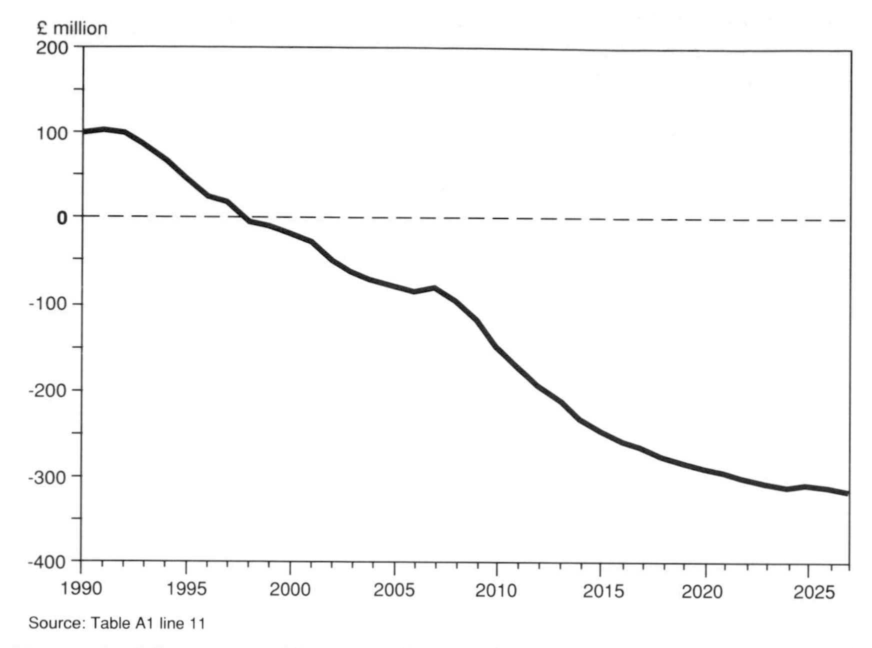


Figure 4 Effect on public expenditure using Treasury funds and collecting repayments via National Insurance

NICs are predictable and with small leakages, the banks could act in sensible insurance terms. They would not need a 100 per cent guarantee but only a fractional guarantee slightly greater than the expected leakage. In Treasury terms this is possible because the risk of leakages above 12 per cent fall *not* on the Treasury but on the banks.

Case 3 illustrates the effect of a fractional guarantee. Students borrow from private-sector funds and repay via NICs, and the Treasury gives banks a guarantee of 12 per cent of outstanding loans, based on a 10 per cent leakage rate. This case is shown by lines 14–16 in Table A1 and by the bottom line in Figure 5, whose calculation is explained in the Notes to Table A1. The effect is dramatic. Net public-sector outlays on the loan scheme in the early years are positive (e.g. £20.4 million in 1990) but are more than offset by the savings on grant and social security benefits (lines 2 and 3 of Table A1). The bottom line in Figure 5 shows that the scheme saves public spending *from the first year onwards*, and in the long run saves around £350 million per year, i.e. more than 40 per cent of expenditure currently on student maintenance. The savings shown by the bottom line in Figure 5 can be used to expand higher education without *any* increase in public spending.

**Private funds with no guarantee** With the fractional guarantee just described, the Treasury takes on the risk up to 12 per cent and the banks the entire risk thereafter. Alternatively, since the risk is small and predictable, it might be simpler if the Treasury were simply to give the banks each year a sum equal to 12 per cent of new loans but no guarantee at all.

This is Case 4: the banks take on the entire risk, for which the Treasury pays what is, in effect, an insurance premium of 12 per cent. This is the sort of commercial risk to which banks are used; it gives the Treasury the advantage of certainty; and it avoids the need for a guarantee, so that the Ryrie rules need not come into play at all. The implications of this arrangement for public spending differ only slightly from those of Case 3. Here the Treasury's actual expenditure each year is precisely 12 per cent, so that the numbers in lines 14–16 of Table A1 apply exactly; in Case 3, if actual leakages are smaller than 12 per cent, actual repayments will be slightly larger than shown in line 15, and the public expenditure savings in Figure 5 will be correspondingly greater.

Case 5 is a variant of Case 4: here the entire risk is taken on by the DES and/or the banks. The Treasury includes in the DES vote an annual sum equal to the expected level of leakage. The DES would then be responsible for reimbursing bank losses (the DES guarantee to the banks could in principle be 100 per cent of losses or, preferably, some much smaller figure). The DES would thus assume any risk out of its own budget. Anything unspent could go into the DES Access Funds set up by the White Paper (UK, 1988, paras 3.21–3.25). The process would be administratively simple and would give the Treasury certainty. It also rather nicely puts moral pressure on graduates to repay.

In conclusion, if the repayment mechanism reduces leakages sufficiently, it should be possible (a) to obtain start-up funds from the private sector and (b) to satisfy the lending institutions with only a fractional guarantee. The result is public-expenditure savings from the very first year, and considerable long-run savings, opening the possibility of early expansion without any additional public spending. The National Insurance mechanism, in short, minimises both the cost of the scheme and the fraction which needs to be guaranteed.

## 4.5 The True Costs of the White Paper

The White Paper estimates of the effects of the loan scheme on public spending, shown in Figure 3, have already been discussed. One reason why the savings are not larger is because of the 25 per cent combined rate of default and write-off. The analysis of section 3 suggests that this is unlikely to be an exaggeration. The case against the White Paper is strong enough even without disputing its cost calculations. This section shows the extent to which its figures understate the true costs. The detailed figures are given in Appendix 1, and the method of calculation is set out in the Explanatory Notes at the end of Table A1 in sufficient detail to allow readers to work out the cost of alternative schemes. The cost figures are summarised in Table 1. This section is written to be self-contained, and can be read without reference to the Appendix.

**Unnecessary and omitted costs in the White Paper** There are two grounds for criticising the White Paper cost figures. First, the leakage of 25 per cent is unnecessarily high, mainly because repayments are collected by banks. Section 3 argued that where repayment is collected by employers via graduates' NICs the combined leakage through default and write-off is unlikely to exceed 10 per cent of outstanding loans.

A second criticism is that the figures in the White Paper omit two additional costs—of administration and of the implied interest subsidy. Taking administrative costs first, it was estimated in section 3 that it would cost banks an average of £100 per student per year to administer loan repayments. Given current student numbers, the total cost of administering the loans of the first three-year cohort is in the region of £50 million per year.

To those students, however, must be added the costs of future cohorts, since administrative costs continue after graduation. Some students will repay within the ten years envisaged in the White Paper (though, it can be argued, a declining number as the size of the loan increases over time). Others will still not have repaid when the loan is written off after 25 years. If the average repayment period is 15 years (i.e. closer to the ten years than the 25 years) then banks will be administering the loans of the equivalent of five three-year cohorts of students, at a total cost, once the loan scheme has been running for that length of time, of around £250 million *per year*. This is not implausible, the more so if one remembers that those graduates who stay in the repayment system longest would be the most expensive cases; i.e. the addition to costs of graduates who take longer to repay exceeds the savings via those who repay within ten years.

In addition to administrative costs, it is necessary to consider also the interest subsidy. The White Paper proposes repayments indexed to the rate of inflation, but with no interest. Real interest rates (i.e. the excess of the rate of interest over the rate of inflation) on average are between 3 and 4 per cent. The rate of return currently on long-run indexed government bonds, depending on the precise method of calculation, is between 3.5 and 3.8 per cent. Thus the White Paper's zero real interest rate represents an untargeted subsidy which is both inefficient and inequitable (see Chapter 3.3).

The cost of the subsidy has to be calculated on the outstanding debt at any time. Since the cumulative total rises to between £7.5 and £8 billion (Table A1, line 33), the cost of a 1 per cent interest subsidy (line 35) rises to a peak of over £75 million per year.

The interest subsidy has a direct bearing on administrative costs. The figure of £250 million per year just discussed assumes that take-up will approach 100 per cent, rather than the 80 per cent assumed in the White Paper. The 100 per cent figure is much the more plausible. First of all, take-up will rise over time as the grant is partly phased out. Much more important, the interest subsidy in the White Paper will from the first lead to take-up of close to 100 per cent: poor students will borrow because they need the money; and rich students will borrow to earn the difference between a zero real interest rate and the positive real return they can make from a Building Society or on the stock market.

**The effect on public spending** of including these additional costs is shown in Table A1, which is only as accurate as the numbers in the White Paper, on which it is based. What can be claimed is that the numbers in Table A1, shown in Figures 5 and 6, are better estimates than the White Paper's calculations, shown in Figure 3.

Line 20 in Table A1 shows administrative costs rising from 1991 onwards with rising numbers of student borrowers. During the 1990s costs rise from below £20 million in the early 1990s (ignoring initial set-up costs), to over £150 million by the turn of the century. By 2005 the scheme will have been running for fifteen years after which, by assumption, new students entering the system will be matched by old students dropping out. Thus after 2005 the cumulative number of students with outstanding loans remains broadly constant, and administrative costs hold steady at £250 million per year.

The cost of a 1 per cent interest subsidy, in contrast, does not peak, but continues to rise as total outstanding loans (Table A1, line 33) rise. If banks require an interest payment of 2 per cent from the government, the effect on public spending rises from around £50 million per year at the turn of the century to £100 million in 2010; by 2025 the cost is over £150 million per year.

The true cost of the White Paper is shown in Figure 5. The benchmark is line (1), which shows the public expenditure cost of the loan scheme claimed by the White Paper; line (2) includes administrative costs in addition to default and write-off, but leaves out the interest subsidy. The effect on public spending (line (2) in Table 1) starts from the White Paper figure of £102 million in 1990 and then (in contrast with the White Paper) rises steadily to a peak of £214 million in 2005. What is going on is that rising administrative costs as more students enter the system outweigh the savings of the loan scheme. After 2005, administrative costs stop rising, and the savings of the loan scheme start to reduce the public expenditure cost, which declines to around £20 million after 2025. *The combined effect of default, write-off and administrative costs wholly outweighs any public expenditure savings*. It would be cheaper simply to give students the money. As discussed in Chapter 3.2, a Swedish government committee on their (private sector) loan scheme reached the same conclusion.

Matters become even worse when the additional cost of the interest subsidy is added, as shown by the top line in Figure 5 and by line (3) in Table 1. The cost rises from £105 million in 1990 to a peak of £300 million in 2007. Thereafter the figure is reduced by the rising stream of repayments, but the additional public spending never falls below £175 million. *Properly accounting for all costs, the White Paper scheme increases public spending by £300 million in 2005 and in the long run by £180 million per year.*

In rather sharp contrast, the NI scheme reduces public spending by £300 million in 2005 (line (4) of Table 1, shown graphically by the bottom line in Figure 5) and in the long run by £350 million. *The difference in public spending between the White Paper and the NI scheme is nearly £600 million in 2005, and in the long run is over £525 million per year,* as shown by line (5) in Table 1 and graphically by the difference between the top and bottom lines

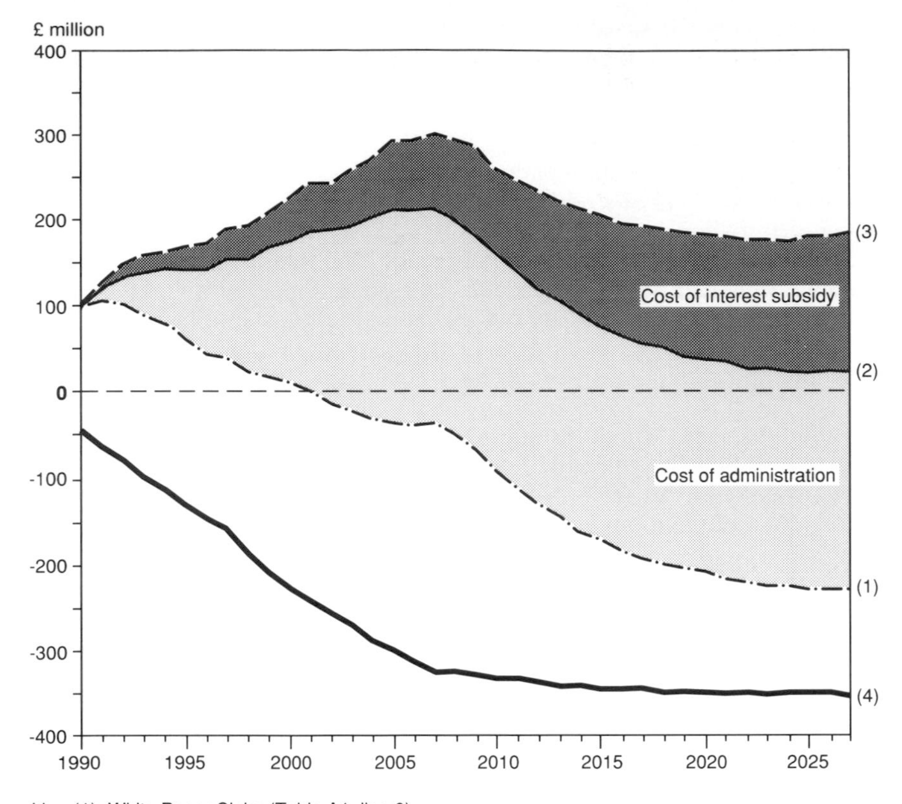


Figure 5 True public expenditure costs of the White Paper and National Insurance schemes

in Figure 5. Put another way, the area between the top and bottom lines in Figure 5 represents public expenditure wasted by the White Paper scheme, which under the NI scheme could be used for expansion.

**Cumulative effects** The magnitude of these numbers is staggering. The claimed savings of the White Paper between 1990 and 2027 are around £3.1 billion (line (1) of Table 1); and of that small saving, £2½ billion (i.e. about 80 per cent) is the result of the withdrawn social security benefits.

The £3.1 billion figure, as we have seen, is illusory. The Secretary of State for Education, in commending the White Paper to the House of Commons (*Hansard* (Commons), 9 November 1988, cols 305–8) stated that the scheme increased public spending by £850 million in the period to 2002.[8] Adding administrative costs raises the figure to over £2½ billion, i.e. the true

TABLE 1: SUMMARY OF PUBLIC EXPENDITURE AND REAL RESOURCE EFFECTS OF THE WHITE PAPER[a,b]

| | 1990 | 1995 | 2000 | 2005 | 2010 | 2015 | 2020 | 2027 | TOTAL |
|---|---|---|---|---|---|---|---|---|---|
| EFFECTS ON PUBLIC SPENDING (Figs 3 & 5) | | | | | | | | | |
| (1) White Paper | 102 | 59 | 11 | –36 | –92 | –174 | –210 | –229 | –3088 |
| (2) White Paper incl admin costs | 102 | 143 | 178 | 214 | 158 | 76 | 40 | 21 | 4497 |
| (3) White Paper incl admin costs and interest subsidy | 105 | 167 | 226 | 290 | 264 | 203 | 183 | 183 | 7927 |
| (4) NIC scheme | –45 | –130 | –228 | –301 | –333 | –344 | –350 | –352 | –10,357 |
| (5) PSBR saving of NIC scheme compared with White Paper (=4–3) | –150 | –297 | –454 | –591 | –597 | –547 | –533 | –535 | –18,284 |
| REAL RESOURCE EFFECTS (Fig 6) | | | | | | | | | |
| (6) Admin saving of NIC scheme | 0 | –74 | –157 | –240 | –240 | –240 | –240 | –240 | –7135 |
| (7) Reduced leakage and interest subsidy | –3 | –37 | –76 | –118 | –161 | –199 | –222 | –244 | –5278 |
| (8) Real resource savings of NIC scheme (=6+7) | –3 | –111 | –233 | –358 | –401 | –439 | –462 | –484 | –12,413 |

NOTES [a] £ million. All costs are positive numbers, all savings are negative.
[b] Rounded to nearest whole number.

SOURCE Table A1 (see also the Explanatory Notes to Table A1)
Line 1 = Table A1, line 6.
Line 2 = Table A1, line 21.
Line 3 = Table A1, line 22.
Line 4 = Table A1, line 16.
Line 6 = Table A1, line 31.
Line 7 = Table A1, line 30 – (2 × line 35).
TOTAL = cumulative total, 1990–2027.

increase in public spending between 1990 and 2002 is three times the White Paper figure.

Comparing the true costs of the White Paper (line (3) of Table 1) with those of the NIC scheme (line (4)) highlights the White Paper's deficiencies even more strongly. From the last column of Table 1, *the cumulative addition to public spending between 2001 and 2010 if the White Paper scheme is implemented instead of the NIC scheme is £5.7 billion, and between 1990 and 2027, £18.3 billion*. These numbers are calculated simply by summing across the relevant lines in Table A1; if account were taken of the interest on the additional borrowing, the figures would be even larger. As a device for saving public spending the White Paper scheme is not a great success.

**Real resource effects of the National Insurance scheme** The effect of the loan scheme on the size of the public sector is one aspect. Another is the cost in real resources of the White Paper proposals compared with the NI scheme. The figures below are not about taxation and borrowing; they measure the real resources used by the White Paper scheme which are not used in the NI scheme and which, in the latter case, are available for other uses.

The saving on administrative costs is of particular importance, in that these are resources which the White Paper scheme literally tips down the drain, i.e. resources of manpower and equipment which are wholly wasted. The saving is the difference between the cost of administering the White Paper scheme and that of administering the NI scheme. For the reasons given in Chapter 5.6, the extra DSS costs of assisting employers to collect graduate repayments are very small, probably in the region of £10 million per year. The resulting savings are shown in line (6) of Table 1.

Two other effects—the reduced leakage and the smaller interest subsidy—are different. They measure the resources going to graduates which, in terms of efficiency and equity, should be extracted from them to reflect the private benefit of a degree. If the loan scheme is genuine, with a self-perpetuating fund, such resources should be spent on future generations of students. If the loan fund is not reimbursed, the sums involved are a gratuitous transfer from future generations of students to the present generation; alternatively, if the loan fund is reimbursed out of government revenues, the transfer is from taxpayers.

Some leakage is necessary and desirable (e.g. the unpaid loans of graduates with low earnings); what is being attacked here is that the White Paper scheme contains *unnecessary* leakages and subsidies, which are inefficient (e.g. the interest subsidy) and whose distributional consequences are arbitrary (unnecessary defaults) or regressive (the interest subsidy). This aspect of the White Paper violates Principle 6 in Chapter 3.4 (see also the discussion in Chapter 3.3).

The reduction in the interest subsidy depends, first, on the extent to which the NI scheme makes it easier to charge graduates a positive rate of interest. The calculations in Chapter 5.2 show that an extra NIC of $1\frac{1}{4}$ pence in the pound would be sufficient to repay an indexed loan equal to half the

London grant over 25 years at a 2 per cent real rate of interest. Since this is 2 per cent more than the White Paper charges, that is the minimum saving. A second factor is that, with the more secure repayments of the NI scheme, banks might be prepared to charge a lower interest rate, though this effect might be offset by the government's ability to borrow more cheaply than the private sector. The discussion which follows assumes that the NI scheme requires 2 per cent less subsidy than the White Paper scheme, an assumption which is kind to the White Paper. The resulting savings, together with those from reduced leakages, are shown by line (7) in Table 1.

**Magnitude of the savings** The resource effects of the White Paper proposal in comparison with the NI scheme are thus (a) substantially higher administrative costs, (b) avoidable default and write-offs totalling about 15 per cent of outstanding loans, and (c) an extra 2 per cent interest subsidy. The resource effects of the NI scheme in comparison with the White Paper scheme are shown in Figure 6. The area between the horizontal axis and line (1) shows the effect of reduced default and write-off, which rise from £12 million in 1995 to £55 million in 2010 and to over £80 million in 2025.

Line (2) adds the administrative savings, which rise steadily from around £75 million in the mid-1990s to £150 million at the turn of the century, and

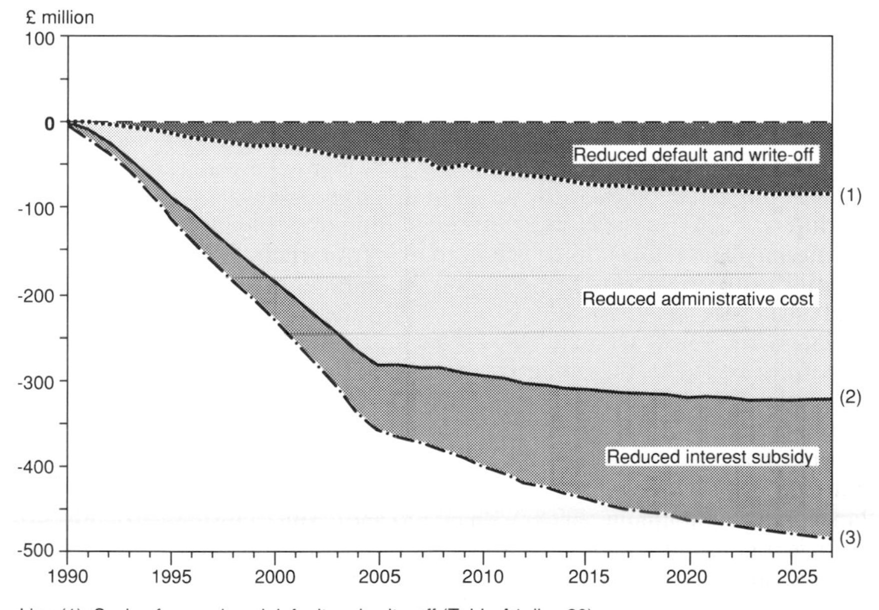


Figure 6 Real resource effects of the National Insurance scheme compared with the White Paper scheme

to £240 million in 2005, after which, as discussed earlier, they remain constant.

The bottom line shows the total resource effects of the NI scheme, including the interest subsidy, compared with the White Paper scheme. The pattern is similar to line (2) until 2005, when costs (line (8) of Table 1) are £360 million; thereafter, since the cost of the interest subsidy continues to rise, total costs increase to £400 million in 2010, and to £480 million in 2025.

Again, the cumulative figures are noteworthy. In administrative resources alone the NI scheme saves about £2¼ billion between 2001 and 2010, and over the whole period to 2027, over £7 billion. Including the effects of reduced leakages and lower interest subsidy, the figures are £3.5 billion for the sub-period, and nearly £12.4 billion for the years to 2027. Again, the interest on extra public-sector borrowing has been ignored.

## 4.6 Conclusion

The White Paper is fundamentally flawed. It is probably wrong in totally excluding students from housing benefit; it fails to raise the incomes of quite a few students, disproportionately those who most need an increase; and it erodes the differential grant for mature students, London students and students from the least well-off backgrounds who currently receive the full grant.

Additional problems include the adverse labour-supply effects caused by the 85 per cent 'spike' in Option A (see section 2), and the arbitrary transfers due to the interest subsidy and to the unnecessarily large defaults and write-offs.

The strategic problem with the White Paper is that its cost calculations just do not add up; the costs are so huge that they rule out any prospect of expanding higher education, even in the very long run. There are two issues: judged in its own terms, the costs of the White Paper scheme (line (3) of Table 1) are enormous; entirely separately, the savings of the NI scheme (line (4) of Table 1) are roughly as large again. When the costs of the White Paper are added to the potential savings of the NI scheme the results are dramatic. The difference is shown graphically in Figure 5: the costs above the zero line are the true addition to public spending of the White Paper scheme, the savings below the line are those of the NI scheme. The difference between the two (line (5) of Table 1) rises from £150 million in 1990 to nearly £600 million in 2005, with a long-run difference of around £525 million. Put another way, *adopting the NI scheme in place of the White Paper scheme reduces public spending in the long run by over £500 million per year. The cumulative savings between 1990 and 2027 are over £18 billion.*

The real resource effects are equally dramatic, as shown in Figure 6. The administrative saving alone from 2005 onwards is around £240 million per year. The total resource effects of the NIC scheme (line (8) of Table 1) exceed £350 million per year by 2005, and are well in excess of £450 million per year by 2020. These resources (and especially the administrative saving) should be put to other uses, most particularly the expansion of higher education.

However one looks at it, the White Paper scheme is a horrendously leaky bucket, and quite unnecessarily so. This is not simply an argument of principle. As Table 1 and Figures 5 and 6 show, the numbers involved are huge. If the White Paper scheme were all that were on offer, there is no question that it would be vastly cheaper simply to give the students the money. Since one of the Treasury's main tasks is to see that taxpayers get value for money, the National Insurance scheme is clearly one they should welcome.

# 5 National Insurance Based Loans

## 5.1 The Basic Idea

**Different types of income-contingent loan schemes** Student loans must have income-related repayments (see the quotes by Robbins and Blaug in Chapter 1.3). Thus it is vital to choose Option D (UK, 1988, para 3.15). Loans of this type can vary along two dimensions. They can be organised via *income tax* or via *National Insurance Contributions* (NICs). There is a strong presumption that administrative costs are minimised when a small scheme (i.e. student loans) is 'piggy-backed' onto a larger one like income tax or the National Insurance system.

The second dimension is whether the scheme is organised as a loan or as a graduate tax. Under a loan scheme the student repays what he/she has borrowed until the loan (plus interest) has been paid off, at which point repayment ceases. With a graduate tax repayments are for life, or until some predetermined date such as the age of retirement. Graduate taxes thus redistribute from rich graduates to poor; pure loan schemes do not. Each approach is internally consistent; either is possible, and either can be supported; but it is important not to muddle the two.

Though these ingredients can be put together into different packages, the scheme suggested here is very specific: it is a genuine loan scheme with repayments organised via NICs.

**Loans to replace parental contributions** The starting point is to phase out parental contributions. The method is best shown by example. The full London grant in 1989/90 is £2650. Students would still be assessed for a parental contribution; however, they would be told that they could now take out a loan equal to the assessed parental contribution, up to a maximum of £1325 (i.e. half the grant). The decision whether or not to take out a loan would be the student's (i.e. there is nothing compulsory about the scheme). The effect would be to abolish at a stroke all assessed parental contributions of less than half the grant. And for the best-off parents it would halve the parental contribution, with the promise of total abolition once the scheme was fully in place.

Alternatively, since students need a boost to their incomes, it would be possible to adopt the above procedure with two changes: some parental contribution would still be required; and students could be allowed to borrow so as to take their total income to (say) £500 above the current full grant, thus raising their total income by about 20 per cent.

**Repayment** would be via an additonal NIC paid by all individuals who had taken out a loan. For the majority of graduates this would be through the Class I employee contribution. For the self-employed the addition would be applied to the Class IV contribution (but would not be eligible for the Class IV partial tax relief). The calculations in section 2 all relate to the Class I contribution. As a later policy option there could be an additional employer NIC for students graduating after September 1990.

It is worth pointing out immediately the appropriateness of the National Insurance system for collecting repayments, not just because it is administratively cheap, but also because student loans, in that they enable students to redistribute over their lifetime, are very properly part of the Beveridge set-up (a point discussed further in section 8). In addition, no new precedent is created as regards hypothecation: National Insurance Contributions are themselves hypothecated; and hypothecation of some of the resulting revenues already takes place, e.g. the contribution from the National Insurance Fund to the National Health Service. Nor is any administrative precedent raised. Section 6 suggests that graduates pay a slightly higher rate of NIC; the administrative mechanism is exactly the same as for individuals who are contracted out of the state earnings-related pension scheme (SERPS), and therefore pay a lower contribution over certain income ranges.

**The source of funds** should be the private sector to the maximum extent possible so that Treasury funds can be used to expand higher education. Ways of achieving this are discussed in section 3.

**Administration** could be public or private. The disbursement of loans could be organised by central government (the DES or the Department of Social Security (DSS)) or by local authorities (as the grant is currently). Alternatively the distribution of loans could be organised in the private sector by banks or by higher education institutions. Section 6 discusses how these arrangements could be administered.

The system set out in this chapter is very flexible. The various options are described in section 7, though many will not be relevant at the time the scheme is implemented, but could be set in place later. Chapter 6 concludes by setting out a very simple, specific scheme which could start more or less immediately.

## 5.2 The Arithmetic of the Scheme

**The arithmetic** is very hopeful. Table 2 shows the extra NICs necessary to repay £1000 over 10, 15, 20 and 25 years at different rates of interest, assuming that the average earnings of all graduates over their working life are around the national average. The calculations are simple. A loan of £1000 can be repaid over 25 years at a 2 per cent rate of interest with annual repayments of £51.22. If average earnings are £12,000, an extra contribution of 0.43 pence in the pound will yield £51.22.

For reasons of efficiency and also to prevent the arbitrary redistributive effects of inflation, the loan should be indexed; and there should be no substantial interest subsidy. The desirability of both features was argued in Chapter 3.3. It is worth reminding ourselves that what is being proposed is a genuine loan and not a graduate tax. The loan scheme, of itself, is distributionally neutral; distributive goals are achieved more effectively by giving disadvantaged students a larger grant so that they do not need a loan, or require only a small one, in line with Principle 5 (Chapter 3.4).

Since a degree is a lifelong investment it should be possible for an individual to spread repayment over a long period. Given the repayment mechanism there is no argument against the standard 20 to 25 years involved in house purchase (another durable investment).

This points towards a loan in which the principal is indexed to changes in the price level, with a 2 or 3 per cent interest rate and repaid over 25 years. If we assume that (a) the base for NICs and (b) earnings both keep pace with inflation we can ignore inflation and use the figures in Table 2.

TABLE 2: ADDITIONAL NATIONAL INSURANCE CONTRIBUTION (pence per £1) PER £1000 BORROWED[a, b]

| | 10 years | 15 years | 20 years | 25 years |
|---|---|---|---|---|
| INTEREST RATE | | | | |
| 0 per cent | 0.83 | 0.56 | 0.42 | 0.33 |
| 2 per cent | 0.93 | 0.65 | 0.51 | 0.43 |
| 3 per cent | 0.98 | 0.70 | 0.56 | 0.48 |
| 5 per cent | 1.08 | 0.80 | 0.67 | 0.59 |

NOTES: [a] Per £1000 borrowed; compound, monthly repayments, loan indexed to changes in retail prices.
[b] The calculations assume that the average earnings of graduates is £12,000 per year (i.e. about the national average).

**Alternative methods of calculating repayments** Method 1 makes direct use of Table 2. An indexed loan with a 2 per cent interest rate can be repaid over 25 years by an extra NIC of 0.43 pence in the pound per £1000 borrowed.

This, however, is a very conservative figure. Historically earnings and the base on which NICs are paid have both risen in real terms by 2 per cent a year or more. It follows that a repayment of *x* per cent of earnings will rise in *real* terms (i.e. over and above the rate of inflation) by 2 per cent a year or more. Method 2 makes use of this fact. If we expect earnings to rise by 2 per cent each year we can use the top line in Table 2. In other words, a repayment of 0.33p per pound with real income growth of 2 per cent will yield as much over 25 years as would a repayment of 0.43p (in the second line of Table 2) with no growth in real income. An indexed loan of £1000 can thus be repaid over 25 years by an extra NIC of 0.33 pence. Appendix 2 shows the precise way in which this arrangement works, including the time path of repayments for a specific numerical example.

It is highly plausible for at least three reasons to predict that a graduate's real earnings will rise on average by at least 2 per cent per year: earnings overall will rise because of economic growth; the earnings of individual graduates will rise with promotion; and the earnings of graduates will rise as skilled labour becomes increasingly scarce for demographic reasons.

**Some possibilities** Using the growth-based figure (Method 2) of 0.33 pence, half the grant for a three-year degree could be replaced by an extra NIC of $1\frac{1}{4}$ pence; in the long run, *75 per cent of the London grant could be replaced by an extra NIC of 2 pence in the pound.* If this were shared between the graduate and his/her employer, each would pay an extra penny in the pound. For non-London students the figures would be even lower.

## 5.3 Private-Sector Start-Up Funds and the Role of Industry

**Start-Up funds** Any loan scheme will run a deficit in its early years, when students are borrowing but not yet repaying to any great extent. One of the great advantages of the NI scheme, as explained in Chapter 4.5, is that it can be introduced at low public-expenditure cost through the use of private-sector funds to start the scheme.

With secure repayments, banks would be more than prepared to lend to students and, as argued in Chapter 4.4, this should be possible under Ryrie rules without a 100 per cent guarantee. The possibility of the banking sector as a source of funds is realistic in this case precisely because banks are not called on to collect repayments.

A second and additional source of private-sector funds is a user charge on those who employ graduates (an increasingly scarce resource in the 1990s), through an additional employer NIC of 1p in the pound for anyone graduating after April 1990. Depending on the precise assumptions about the number of graduates each year and their average earnings, the yield in the first full year could be between £12 and £14 million. In the second year, with a second cohort of students, the yield would at least double, and so on. If the charge were levied in respect of all students graduating after April 1990, the yield of the employer contribution would rapidly become substantial.

**The importance of private-sector funds** In terms of economic theory it should not matter from which sector students borrow. Suppose it is efficient to expand higher education, and that students borrow from public funds. If additional public borrowing 'crowds out' private investment, it will only be less-efficient private investment which is crowded out—a result which is itself efficient (see Buiter, 1985).

That theoretical conclusion, however, is valid only in a world where both government and taxpayers are wholly rational and have perfect knowledge about the future. Neither is true. Treasury funding requires that taxation is higher than would otherwise be the case, with possible disincentive effects; and higher public spending may have adverse effects in financial and foreign-exchange markets. If students borrow from private funds, no issue of taxation or incentives arises—we do not, after all, argue that the large and growing mortgage debt discourages work effort.

There are also political issues. To the extent that the loan scheme is privately funded, there is no need for a battle between the DES and the Treasury every time it is proposed to extend the scheme to a new class of student. More fundamentally, there is virtually unanimous support for the principle of academic freedom, and considerable support for the view that excessive reliance on Treasury funding threatens that freedom (Robbins himself warned against the dangers if universities received more than half of their income from government sources). It follows that the use of private-sector loan funds, by diversifying the sources of funding, contributes to the independence of higher education, an outcome which is all the more desirable given the conflict within government described in Chapter 1.4.

Thus there are powerful arguments in both economic and political terms for the use of private-sector funds. The resulting savings in public expenditure are huge. Under the NI scheme public spending is nearly £600 million lower than the White Paper scheme in 2005, and the cumulative public-expenditure savings, as discussed in Chapter 4.5, exceed £18 billion. Why does this matter? It matters, first, because the use of private-sector funds on this scale releases public-sector resources which could be used, at least in part, to expand higher education. This is an area in which a properly-organised partnership between government and the private sector can be fruitful.

Second and separately, the loan scheme could expand easily to meet growing student demand. If banks receive a secure return at close to a market interest rate they will be content for the scheme to grow, just as mortgage lending has been able to grow over the years without any worries about its implications for public spending. The scheme suggested here has the same possibilities for expansion.

**Expansion possibilities** If the loan scheme in the long run halves the taxpayer cost of student maintenance this does not mean that we can double the number of students with no increase in public spending; such an argument ignores the cost to the taxpayer of running universities and polytechnics, which would rise if student numbers increased.

The logic of expansion at a constant level of public spending is as follows. If the loan system saves £350 million per year (the long-run figure in line (4) of Table 1, illustrated by the lower half of Figure 5), that amount can be spent each year on expansion without raising public spending. Expenditure on higher education other than on student maintenance is currently about £2.4 billion; if half of the maintenance grant remains, total public spending on higher education is around £2.8 billion. £350 million is about $12\frac{1}{2}$ per cent of expenditure on universities and polytechnics, so that savings from the loan system could finance an increase in places of that magnitude with no net addition to public spending; if the unit of resource (i.e. real expenditure per student) were allowed to decline (drawing a veil over whether or not that would be a good idea) expansion could be greater.

There could be further expansion if the loan were allowed to exceed half the grant. Suppose that in the long run the loan replaced 75 per cent of the grant, and was repaid by an extra penny in the pound each for graduate and employer. The resulting savings are £525 million per year, enough to finance a 20 per cent increase in student numbers.

**The role of industry** We saw in Chapter 1.3 that the three main groups who benefit from higher education are the students themselves, their employers and society at large through the external effects of education. Thus there is a case on efficiency grounds that employers should make a continuing contribution to higher education—a case which is strengthened by demographic prospects.

The possibility of industry contributing some of the start-up funds has been discussed already. A different role (and the two roles could be operated consecutively) is through an additional employer NIC, say of an extra penny in the pound. It might be desirable to impose such a charge irrespective of the graduate's loan status.

The additional contribution is efficient in two ways. First, it forces employers to face the costs of the trained brainpower they hire (given the demographic prospects, an increasingly scarce resource). It might be argued that the employer contribution will be passed on to the consumer in (very slightly) increased prices. That, too, is efficient: it makes consumers face the costs of the scarce resources involved. It is efficient if a poor coffee harvest drives up the price of coffee; and it is efficient if employers, and through them consumers, pay higher prices after a poor brain harvest.

The additional employer contribution also helps to minimise an important market failure. When the government seeks contributions from industry for City Technology Colleges, individual firms are reluctant to contribute because they can see no individual benefit. Each firm has an incentive to be a 'free rider'. The additional employer NIC entirely avoids the free-rider problem: a firm pays what is, in effect, a user charge, and pays it only for those graduates who are contributing to its profits, and whom it wishes to continue to employ.

It will, no doubt, be argued that such a contribution will reduce the competitiveness of British industry. There are at least two responses. First, the imposition is considerably smaller than that imposed on banks by the White Paper. Second, the additional contribution, since it goes back into higher education, is productive. The additional employer contribution, in short, is efficient in both static and dynamic terms. In addition, an extra 1p employer NIC, if levied only up to the upper earnings limit,[1] will cost the employer no more than £170 per year; the sums involved are thus small and unlikely to cause dissension in the ranks.

## 5.4 Costs and Savings

Costs arise in principle in three ways: through default, through write-offs and through emigration. Defaults and write-offs were discussed in Chapter 4.3. All that need be added is that the scheme proposed here is *not* a graduate tax but a genuine loan scheme (see section 1 for the distinction). The solution to leakages, therefore, is not to try to recoup them from richer graduates, but to finance them (either in full, or sharing the risk with the private sector) out of general tax revenues.

Turning to emigration, the first solution is to note that an extra NIC of $1\frac{1}{4}$p will not *cause* graduates to migrate,[2] so that it would not be costly to ignore emigration and include it in write-offs. The second solution is to include in the conditions of the loan a clause converting it into a mortgage-type debt upon emigration, enforced through foreign courts if desired (this is the only solution offered by the White Paper scheme). A third and more stringent form of enforcement, unique to the NI scheme, notes that it would be possible to attach the past contributions or future benefits of a defaulting emigrant. If this were done (and it can be argued that it is not necessary) the only people to escape would be emigrating 21 year olds who never returned. Again, the public-expenditure cost is likely to be small.

For all the reasons discussed here and in Chapter 4, the long-run, steady-state savings of the scheme are enormous compared with the White Paper scheme. These savings allow expansion in the 1990s when it is needed most, and by the early 2000s could be large enough to offer in addition net savings in public expenditure.

## 5.5 Incentive Issues

In principle, income-related repayments avoid the 'spikes' discussed in Chapter 4.2. NICs do not wholly avoid the problem, however, because there is a small 'spike' at the lower earnings limit.[3] This is unfortunate but not devastating. Though the problem is unavoidable, it is vastly smaller than the 85 per cent 'spike' in the White Paper scheme.

Apart from the 'spike' at the lower earnings limit, the extra NIC of $1\frac{1}{4}$p is small enough to avoid labour supply disincentives; all that is happening, after all, is that graduates are giving up part of the 2p income tax cut of the 1988 budget.

If 75 per cent of the maintenance grant were replaced by a loan, the extra contribution would be only 2p for a three-year degree, or 1p each for the graduate and his/her employer. Even if the incidence of the employer contribution were substantially on the graduate there is no evidence of any substantial disincentive; and for graduates above the upper earnings limit, the extra NICs take the form of a lump-sum tax, whose distortionary effect is minimal.

As a separate point, NI-based loans, in contrast with mortgage-type loans, do not distort the choice of degree subject or subsequent job.

Finally, note that the proposals in this chapter do not depend at all on present institutions, and would carry over very easily to any conceivable reform of NICs short of their total abolition.

## 5.6 Administration

Administration would be simple because input would be necessary on only two occasions: when the extra NIC is 'switched on' when the student takes out a loan; and, years down the road, when it is 'switched off' when the loan has been repaid.

**Cumulation during student days** All students have a National Insurance number or could easily get one.

*Administrative model 1:* at the end of each academic year the lending institution (see below) would make a return to the Department of Social Security (DSS) of the student's total borrowing during the year. A 'flag' (see below) would be put against the student's NI number. This deals automatically with students who do not complete their degree (to avoid incentive problems, failure to complete a qualification is *not* a reason for forgiving the loan).

Students in this model would pay extra NICs on earnings whilst a student. This is administratively simple but not ideal from a policy viewpoint. It would be desirable, if an administratively easy way could be found, of suspending the extra NIC until after graduation.

*Administrative model 2:* in this case, the lending institution keeps cumulative records of the student's borrowing and makes the return to DSS only at the end of his/her student days. This automatically postpones payment until after graduation. It would, however, require a mechanism to deal with students who did not graduate.

**The lending institution** In principle students could borrow from central government (DES or DSS) or through local government, as currently with the maintenance grant and fees. Or the disbursement of loan funds could be by higher-education institutions, who already distribute scholarship and hardship funds, and who will be in charge of running the Access Funds. The argument of section 3, however, is that the needs of expansion are best served through the use of private-sector funds; thus students borrow from banks, who would be repaid from the yield of the extra NICs.

It is worth clarifying what is possible and what is not. Chapters 3 and (especially) 4 argued against a loan scheme in which the private sector was responsible both for disbursing the loans and for collecting repayment. But repayments collected by employers through the National Insurance system are the key ingredient which makes private-sector participation genuinely possible.

**Administrative action 1: switching on** At the end of each academic year the lending institution would report to DSS the student's NI number and the amount he/she had borrowed during the year. Alternatively (and from the point of view of DSS simpler), there could be one cumulative return at the time the student graduated.

DSS would put a 'flag' against the student's NI number. The simplest method would add a suffix G to the NI number of all students who had borrowed (henceforth for short 'graduates', taken to include students who did not graduate). There is an exact analogy with those who currently contract out of the state earnings-related pension, and the administrative mechanism would be exactly the same. Any person with the G suffix would pay extra NICs of (say) $1\frac{1}{4}$p in the pound irrespective of the amount borrowed, and the repayment period would vary.

**During repayment** The employer already makes an annual return to DSS for each employee. *The arrangements suggested here require no extra information to be transmitted.* The DSS computer already keeps individual cumulative account of contributions; it would be a simple programming job to extend the computerised record to include the cumulative loan repayment.

The channelling of the repayments from DSS to the banks could be done in a number of ways. Much the simplest is to aggregate the loans of each bank. Under both the White Paper and the NI schemes, banks do not have the option of refusing loans to any student who qualifies. In consequence, there is no need for banks to keep records on individual loan accounts; instead, banks and the DSS could deal in aggregates.

The way in which this works is best shown by example. Suppose that there are only two banks, each of which cumulates its total lending to students. If bank A has lent a total of £200 million and bank B £100 million, bank A would be entitled to two-thirds and bank B to one-third of the revenue from the extra NIC (boosted from general tax revenues to deal with leakages, as discussed in Chapter 4.4). These sums could be paid by the DSS either to banks A and B directly, or the entire proceeds of the additional NICs could be paid to banks through the clearing mechanism.

From the graduate's point of view, repayment is on a strictly individual basis, with repayment ceasing once the loan plus interest has been paid off; but all repayments are put into a single pool, of which each lending institution receives a proportionate share. This procedure has no efficiency costs and offers enormous administrative simplification.

The fact that banks all draw proportionately from a common repayment stream might make it appear that they are not really lending to individuals at all, but to the government. If so, might such an arrangement fall foul of the Ryrie rules? There are two responses. First, as discussed in Chapter 4.4, the Ryrie rules are relevant only to the extent of any Treasury guarantee; if banks receive a guarantee of up to 10 per cent of outstanding loans, then this is the maximum potential public expenditure.[4] Second, it can be argued that banks are not lending to government, but investing in graduates. Discussion of this latter view is taken up in section 7.

It would, of course, be possible to work on an individual basis, under which the NICs of each graduate were credited to his/her individual loan account. To achieve this, the graduate's bank account would be 'tagged' by his/her NI number, which would serve as the link whereby the DSS computer could talk directly to banks' computers. Such an arrangement is entirely possible, but would involve development of the necessary software; it might also require additional investment in computer capacity. Neither cost is trivial. It should be noted, however, that both take the form of a one-off, start-up cost; once the initial investment is made, the system thereafter would be relatively cheap to run.

**Administrative action 2: switching off** When the student has repaid the loan the DSS computer will so signify. At that stage the employer will be notified that the G suffix has been deleted.

Several points are worth repeating. There are only two administrative episodes; switching on and switching off. In between, everything works automatically using existing computerised administrative machinery and procedures. There is a sharp contrast with, say, mortgage interest relief pre-MIRAS,[5] where tax codes had to be changed every time the interest rate changed (in 1977/8 I had *five* PAYE codes—see Barr, 1977).

Other than switching on and switching off, student loans would not be organised by government at all: the loan would be issued by the banking system; and repayments would be administered by the employer as part of the existing collection of NICs. The only exception is the self-employed, for whom the detailed arrangements via the Class 4 contribution remain to be worked out. All in all, the proposed arrangements are very substantially a private-sector scheme, the desirability of which was discussed in section 3.

## 5.7 Longer-Run Possibilities

The initial scheme should be simple. The idea, however, is very flexible, and could be extended in the long run in all sorts of ways. Some are listed here to illustrate the point; none is essential to the scheme.

**The balance of loan and grant** In the longer term loans could replace more than the parental contribution up to half the grant. The White Paper talks of a long-run balance of 50 per cent grant and 50 per cent loan. Once the loan scheme was in place and bedded down, both technically and in terms of people's perceptions, the loan element could perhaps be increased, with the grant increasingly taking on the function of ensuring a level playing field between different types of student (see Principle 5 in Chapter 3.4). This would be relatively easy with the scheme suggested here, very difficult from every point of view with repayments organised along the lines of Option A.

The balance could be shifted much more easily if repayment were shared between graduates and employers. A contribution by employers to higher education is highly desirable on efficiency grounds (Chapter 1.3 and

Principle 7 in Chapter 3.4); and the National Insurance mechanism offers an administratively easy way of bringing this about. As we have seen, 75 per cent of the London grant could be replaced by an extra penny each for the graduate and his/her employer, and less for the non-London grant.

**Longer degrees and postgraduate qualifications** It would be speculative at this stage to delve too deeply into these matters. But using the growth-based calculation in section 2, an extra NIC of .33p will repay £1000 over 25 years; thus a loan equal to half the (non-London) grant for a four-year Scottish degree would require an extra NIC of 1.4p. A loan equal to half the London grant over five years (e.g. for medical students) would require an extra 2.1p. Or suppose a student took out a loan for half the grant for a three-year degree, plus a full grant for a postgraduate year; again, the extra NIC would be 2.1p. A loan to cover the full London grant for a three-year degree plus a three-year PhD requires additional NICs of around 5p. For all sorts of reasons it would be necessary to place a ceiling on the total amount of additional NIC to which any student could make him/herself liable. What this shows is that the loan scheme *can* be extended to longer periods of study. Whether it *should* be so extended is a matter of policy. It might, for instance, be decided that doctors should not have to incur a substantially larger loan than other students, in which case they could be given some extra grant-type support, possibly from the Department of Health and Social Services.

**Home responsibility protection** Consider the case of a woman who graduates aged 21, marries and has children without going into the labour force. Under the scheme as it stands, interest on her loan continues to clock up. If she joined the workforce aged 35 (which demographics will make very desirable) she might be in a position where she could never repay in full. If this outcome were thought undesirable for reasons of incentives or of equity, existing home responsibility protection could be extended to the interest component of the loan.[6] This would have the effect of 'stopping the clock', and the person concerned would join the labour force at 35 in exactly the same position as if they had joined at 21. For a student borrowing half the non-London grant at a 2 per cent interest rate, the implied subsidy would cost around £65 per person per year. Since it is part of existing home responsibility protection, such payments should come from the National Insurance Fund rather than from general tax revenues.

**Forgiving the loan** It would be possible within the scheme partly or wholly to forgive the loan, either for labour market reasons, e.g. to encourage engineers to stay engineers, for for distributional reasons, e.g. for nurses or primary school teachers. The mechanism could be used to give appropriate incentives: for instance repayments could be suspended (but not forgiven) for the first five years; thereafter 20 per cent (or 10 per cent) of the loan could be forgiven for each further year of service. The entire loan would thus be written off after ten or 15 years.

**Accelerated loan repayments** It bears repetition that this is a genuine loan scheme in which no student repays more than he/she has borrowed. It would therefore be both possible and easy for any student to repay early if he/she so wished; and it would be open to government to give an inducement to early repayment were this thought desirable. Equally, employers could pay off a graduate's loan as a 'golden hello', though it is more likely that they would do so only after the graduate had worked for, say, five years (i.e. a golden glad-that-you-stayed).

**A new type of financial asset** It was suggested in section 6 that though the NICs of individual graduates could be channelled back to their individual loan accounts, it would be administratively vastly cheaper if each bank aggregated its student lending and received a proportionate share of total graduate repayments. Thus if bank A had made half of all outstanding student loans it would be entitled to half of the yield of the extra NICs.

Bank A thus has a claim on half of the yield of (say) $1\frac{1}{4}$ per cent of an earnings stream which will rise over time in line with the increase in real graduate earnings. This claim is a financial asset which can be sold. Depending on the precise way in which repayments are calculated, the asset can represent an equity stake in graduates. Harking back to the discussion in Chapter 3.2, financial markets have not in the past been willing to make long-term loans to students because the loan is unsecured. A theoretical way of giving banks security is to legalise slavery; an equity stake in graduate earnings achieves exactly the same result.

The new financial asset is analogous to the secondary market in mortgages. It has several advantages. It deals with banks' reluctance about having too much long-term debt by giving them the option to have as much or as little long-term involvement in student loans as they want. Pension funds, in contrast, want long-term assets, but the government is currently not selling long-term gilts in any quantity. Viewed as national investment, the asset is efficient given the demographic prospects; and from the viewpoint of individual saving, it is safer than buying cocoa futures.

The asset opens up the (not wholly fanciful) prospect of the National Union of Mineworkers' pension fund owning a stake in the long-term prospects of graduates; retired miners would be living off the sweat of young graduate city analysts. From one viewpoint, this achieves the Tory dream of a shareowning democracy; from another it achieves a socialist dream of the young and rich supporting the elderly and less well-off; from another it would alleviate conflict over pay differentials.

## 5.8 Advantages of the Scheme

Many of the advantages have emerged at least implicitly during earlier discussion, but it is useful to list them systematically (see also the comments by Lords Beloff and Halsbury (*Hansard* (Lords), 9 November 1988, cols 640 and 642).

**The strategy for expansion and access** has two principles. First, start-up funds should come from the private sector, and the saved public expenditure used to expand the system; this contributes to access on the supply side. Second, loans with income-related repayments do not discourage prospective students, thus addressing access on the demand side. Further demand-side policies would be additional assistance for 16–19 year olds, and phasing out the parental contribution. The scheme (unlike mortgage-type arrangements) makes a very substantial contribution to access and expansion.

**Efficiency** The expansion of higher education can be supported in *efficiency* terms, given demographic trends, the single European market and the technological developments underlying the move towards a knowledge-based society. A related advantage is that the scheme can readily be extended to new classes of student, thus avoiding a battle between DES and the Treasury every time expansion is proposed.

Additionally, since the extra NIC is small, job choice is not distorted and labour-supply disincentives are minimal; for those above the upper earnings limit the additional contribution is equivalent to a lump-sum tax, and therefore does not distort job choice or labour supply at all.

Since there is little escape from NICs, repayment can be spread over an extended period, but early repayment is possible. The result, given that something close to a market rate of interest is charged, is to minimise distortions to intertemporal choice.

**Cost** The scheme saves public expenditure from the very first year and is cheap to administer. Defaults are minimal; emigration leakages can be kept small; and the unpaid loans of the low paid (estimated in Chapter 4.3 at about 8 per cent of outstanding loans) are likely to be a declining cost given demographic trends.

Administrative costs will also be small. DSS will have to switch on the additional NIC and, years later, switch it off. In between, administration for the great majority of graduates will be by the employer. The scheme is flexible, and can have additional features added in later years without causing major administrative burdens during the transition.

In terms of defaults, loans written off and administrative costs the scheme is cheaper than the White Paper proposals by amounts which run into hundreds of millions of pounds per year.

**Equity** The scheme is not only efficient and cheap. It is also fair, and seen to be so. It is a loan, not a graduate tax, and so no-one repays more than he/she has borrowed. Equally, however, no-one repays more than they can afford: the unemployed make no repayments, nor do parents working in the home; and graduate nurses make only small repayments, at least early in their career. In the longer term there are options for home responsibility protection and forgiveness of loans in less well-paid jobs.

**Legislative implications** A small but highly important point is that the scheme might well require no additional legislation save a few extra clauses in the 1990 Finance Bill.

**Advantages relative to collection via income tax** The arguments in favour of a loan as opposed to a graduate tax have already been made. In addition, the use of NICs rather than income tax to collect repayments has several advantages.

Since it is earnings which are increased by a degree, it is right that repayment should be based on earnings rather than total (earned plus unearned) income; NICs achieve this automatically.

Second, the upper earnings limit has the major advantage, as mentioned already, that for those above it the extra contribution has all the characteristics of a lump-sum tax.

The upper earnings limit also automatically solves the 'Mick Jagger problem'. If repayment were, say, an extra 2p on a former student's marginal rate of income tax, Mick Jagger (one and a bit years as an LSE undergraduate) could end up single-handedly providing maintenance for the entire UK undergraduate population. Depending on one's viewpoint this is inequitable; it also gives strong incentives to emigration.

NICs are hard to evade; what is more the individual has no incentive to evade since contributions carry entitlement to future benefits.

The use of the National Insurance mechanism also lends itself easily to an employer contribution, a highly desirable policy in efficiency terms, and one which is easy to administer.

Finally, since NICs are levied strictly on an individual basis, the 'negative dowry' problem is solved automatically.

Some of these features could be managed under income tax, but they would require a lot more administrative input. They happen automatically with the National Insurance mechanism.

**Compatibility with the idea of National Insurance** The use of the National Insurance system in this context offers considerable reinforcement to the contributory principle.

Student loans, upon reflection, are very much in keeping with the spirit of the Beveridge system, one of whose main purposes is to enable individuals to be self-sufficient over their lifetime as a whole, by redistributing from themselves at one stage in their life cycle to themselves at another. That is what the National Insurance retirement pension does. Student loans are precisely another such case. The student needs access to his/her future earnings; private capital markets are not able for technical reasons to supply such loans (Chapter 3.2); thus an arrangement which uses the National Insurance mechanism is *efficient*. Student loans are just an up-front pension.

**Political dimensions** Who are the winners and losers? Most graduates will be worse off by about a penny in the pound. *That is the worst loss that will be sustained by anyone*. When students ask why they should pay for something which they have hitherto had free, there are two answers: first, a good loan system will increase their current income; second, and much more important, their additional NICs enable them to share the wealth by improving access for the next generation of students.

This brings us to the winners. They are, first, students currently in poverty because of unpaid parental contributions. Second, are prospective students who do not go into higher education because they know that their parents will not pay their contribution. Under the scheme proposed here, parental contributions can largely be abolished for many parents, and halved instantly for the richest. The scheme thus offers a genuine prospect of Parents Lib; for many students it will also be Students Lib. The scheme will therefore be popular with students; for largely the same reasons, it will also be popular with parents; and, by offering secure repayments at close to a market interest rate, it will be popular with banks.

Finally, and most important of all, are the biggest winners—those many students who currently are unable to get into higher education because places are so scarce.

# 6 Summary and Conclusion

## 6.1 Principles of Student Support

Analysis of student maintenance in Britain and abroad (Chapters 2 and 3) suggests a number of practical lessons, from which can be inferred some broad principles. These are worth repeating briefly.

**Practical lessons** can be summarised in four propositions.

△ The grant system works badly (Chapter 2.2).

△ Expanding the grant system is not the answer (Chapter 2.3).

△ Mortage-type loans will harm access, will be costly in public-expenditure terms and will not allow higher education to expand (Chapter 3.2).

△ The White Paper proposal to collect repayments by the private banking system will be very expensive to administer and costly in terms of defaults and write-offs. These costs rule out any expansion in either the short or the long run (Chapter 4).

**Principles of student support** were set out in Chapter 3.4.

*Principle 1:* Because of its external benefits higher education should continue to receive substantial taxpayer support. But there are also substantial private benefits, and so the individual student should meet part of the cost.

*Principle 2:* Given the problems with parental contributions it is both inefficient and inequitable that students should be *compelled* to depend on their families; the system of student support should reduce such dependence by giving students access to their future earnings.

*Principle 3:* Student support should offer the individual protection against the risk involved in borrowing to finance part of the costs of doing a degree.

From the first three Principles we can derive:

*Principle 4:* Students should finance part of the cost of doing a degree through loans; such loans should have repayments related to the subsequent income of the individual student.

*Principle 5:* Some grant should remain; but its function, increasingly, should be to bring about a level playing field between different groups of students. Thus there should be a larger grant for students from disadvantaged backgrounds, for mature students, and possibly also for students studying in London and those doing longer-than-average degrees.

*Principle 6:* For both efficiency and equity reasons, loans should be indexed; they should also be substantially unsubsidised. Distributive goals should be achieved through the application of Principle 5.

*Principle 7:* Because employers are one of the main beneficiaries, industry should contribute to the cost of higher education.

Finally, student support should be designed as a coherent *strategy*, not as a jumble of *ad hoc* policies.

## 6.2 A Specific Proposal for Immediate Implementation

**Policy aims and how to achieve them** The aims of higher education policy should be to improve access and to enable the system to expand. The strategy for achieving these aims without any increase in public spending has two legs.

△ Start-up funds should come from the private sector, and the savings in public expenditure, at least through the 1990s, used to expand the system; this contributes to access on the supply side.

△ Loans with income-related repayments will not discourage applications, thus addressing access on the demand side. Other demand-side policies include additional assistance for 16–19 year olds and the phasing out of the parental contribution.

**A scheme to start in 1990** Loans with repayment related to the student's subsequent income can be organised via income tax or National Insurance Contributions, and can take the form of a loan or a graduate tax. The proposal in Chapter 5 is for a genuine loan scheme (i.e. one in which no-one repays more than they have borrowed), with repayment collected by employers through the National Insurance system.

Four steps are essential.

(1) Though phasing out parental contributions is desirable, the loan facility in the early days might best be used mainly to boost student incomes, and parental contributions phased out only when that has been achieved.

(2) Start-up funds should come from the private sector. Given that repayment is secure, the source of all or most student borrowing should be the banking system.

(3) The disbursement of loans, and record keeping during student days,

should be administered by the banking system, possibly with the assistance of higher-education institutions.

(4) Repayments are administered for the great majority of graduates by their employers through an extra National Insurance Contribution of between 1 and $1\frac{1}{2}$p for any student who has borrowed from the scheme. On plausible assumptions this extra contribution will repay half the grant over 25 years, assuming an indexed loan and a 2 per cent interest rate.

A fifth component is optional.

(5) There should be a small additional employer National Insurance Contribution for all post-1990 graduates, not only those with loans, so that employers share in the cost of higher education through a user charge for the graduates they employ.

**The advantages** of the scheme are set out in Chapter 5.8.

△The scheme allows substantial saving on student maintenance, and could be introduced in such a way that there are public expenditure savings *from the first year onwards*. The scheme thus offers resources for an immediate expansion of higher education.

△The savings in public expenditure are very large (Chapter 4.5): adopting the National Insurance scheme in place of the White Paper scheme reduces public spending in the long run by over £500 million per year. The cumulative savings between 1990 and 2027 are over £18 billion. Both figures are even larger if the loan is allowed to exceed half the grant. The real resource savings are also substantial. The National Insurance scheme reduces administrative costs by £240 million per year, and by a cumulative total of over £7 billion. It is therefore possible to have sustainable expansion of higher education in the 1990s *and also* Treasury savings in the early 2000s, when the demographic crunch comes.

△The scheme enables parental contributions to be phased out.

△Because the additional National Insurance Contribution is small, labour market distortions are minimal. For those above the upper earnings limit, repayment is equivalent to a lump-sum tax.

△The scheme is fair, and will be seen to be so. No-one repays more than they have borrowed; and with income-related repayments no-one repays more than they can afford.

△The scheme is flexible: it allows early repayment by graduates (or their employers); and it can accommodate a variety of social policy goals such as home responsibility protection, and forgiveness of loans in less well-paid jobs.

△Since students borrow from private-sector sources and since banks receive a reliable return, the scheme is readily extensible to new classes of students (e.g. those studying part time, and those currently eligible only for non-mandatory grants) without the need for a battle between the DES and the Treasury whenever such an extension is proposed.

△ The scheme accords well with a key aspect of the Beveridge philosophy. It reinforces the contributory principle and helps individuals to be self-supporting by enabling them to redistribute to themselves at different stages in their life cycle. This is what retirement pensions do. Student loans are an up-front pension. Since the private market does not readily supply long-term unsecured loans it is *efficient* that there should be some state involvement at least in providing a mechanism for collecting repayments.

The National Insurance loan scheme, in short, is flexible, cheap to run, easy to understand, administratively simple, politically attractive, efficient, fair and easily extensible. It should be part of the 1990 Finance Bill and should take effect in September 1990.

# Appendix 1: The Costs of the White Paper and National Insurance Schemes

TABLE A1: PSBR AND REAL RESOURCE EFFECTS UNDER DIFFERENT ASSUMPTIONS

| 1 | 1990 | 1991 | 1992 | 1993 | 1994 |
|---|---|---|---|---|---|
| **PSBR Effects** | | | | | |
| 2 Net change in grant | 0 | –22 | –42 | –61 | –78 |
| 3 Net change in benefits | –65 | –65 | –64 | –63 | –61 |
| 4 Gross loan outlay | 167 | 193 | 216 | 236 | 255 |
| 5 Gross repayments | 0 | –2 | –9 | –21 | –39 |
| 6 **PSBR White Paper** | **102** | **104** | **101** | **91** | **77** |
| 7 | | | | | |
| 8 | | | | | |
| 9 Gross loan outlay | 167 | 193 | 216 | 236 | 255 |
| 10 Gross repayments | 0 | –2.4 | –10.8 | –25.2 | –46.8 |
| 11 **PSBR 2** | **102** | **103.6** | **99.2** | **86.8** | **69.2** |
| 12 | | | | | |
| 13 | | | | | |
| 14 Gross loan outlay | 20.04 | 23.16 | 25.92 | 28.32 | 30.6 |
| 15 Gross repayments | 0 | –0.288 | –1.296 | –3.024 | –5.616 |
| 16 **PSBR NI Scheme** | **–44.96** | **–64.128** | **–81.376** | **–98.704** | **–114.016** |
| 17 | | | | | |
| 18 | | | | | |
| 19 | | | | | |
| 20 Admin costs | | 17 | 34 | 50 | 67 |
| 21 **PSBR WP + Admin** | **102** | **121** | **135** | **141** | **144** |
| 22 **Line 21 + interest subs** | **105.34** | **128.16** | **146.3** | **156.6** | **163.92** |
| 23 | | | | | |
| 24 Line 22 minus line 16 | 150.3 | 192.288 | 227.676 | 255.304 | 277.936 |
| 25 | | | | | |
| 26 | | | | | |
| 27 **Real Resource Effects** | | | | | |
| 28 | | | | | |
| 29 | | | | | |
| 30 Less leakage | 0 | –0.4 | –1.8 | –4.2 | –7.8 |
| 31 Admin saving | 0 | –7 | –24 | –40 | –57 |
| 32 | | | | | |
| 33 Outstanding loan | 167 | 358 | 565 | 780 | 996 |
| 34 | | | | | |
| 35 1 per cent int. subsidy | –1.67 | –3.58 | –5.65 | –7.8 | –9.96 |
| 36 | | | | | |
| 37 **Resource savings** | **–3.34** | **–14.56** | **–37.1** | **–59.8** | **–84.72** |
| 38 | | | | | |
| 39 W/out interest subs | 0 | –7.4 | –25.8 | –44.2 | –64.8 |

* NOTES: see end of Table, p 78

| 1 | 1995 | 1996 | 1997 | 1998 | 1999 | 2000 | 2001 |
|---|---|---|---|---|---|---|---|
| **PSBR Effects** | | | | | | | |
| 2 | –95 | –112 | –121 | –152 | –172 | –192 | –206 |
| 3 | –59 | –59 | –62 | –63 | –65 | –65 | –65 |
| 4 | 275 | 297 | 324 | 356 | 385 | 410 | 429 |
| 5 | –62 | –83 | –102 | –119 | –131 | –142 | –155 |
| 6 | **59** | **43** | **39** | **22** | **17** | **11** | **3** |
| 7 | | | | | | | |
| 8 | | | | | | | |
| 9 | 275 | 297 | 324 | 356 | 385 | 410 | 429 |
| 10 | –74.4 | –99.6 | –122.4 | –142.8 | –157.2 | –170.4 | –186 |
| 11 | **45.6** | **26.4** | **18.6** | **–1.8** | **–9.2** | **–17.4** | **–28** |
| 12 | | | | | | | |
| 13 | | | | | | | |
| 14 | 33 | 35.64 | 38.88 | 42.72 | 46.2 | 49.2 | 51.48 |
| 15 | –8.928 | –11.952 | –14.688 | –17.136 | –18.864 | –20.448 | –22.32 |
| 16 | **–129.928** | **–147.312** | **–158.808** | **–189.416** | **–209.664** | **–228.248** | **–241.84** |
| 17 | | | | | | | |
| 18 | | | | | | | |
| 19 | | | | | | | |
| 20 | 84 | 100 | 117 | 134 | 150 | 167 | 184 |
| 21 | **143** | **143** | **156** | **156** | **167** | **178** | **187** |
| 22 | **167.18** | **171.46** | **188.9** | **193.64** | **209.72** | **226.08** | **240.56** |
| 23 | | | | | | | |
| 24 | 297.108 | 318.772 | 347.708 | 383.056 | 419.384 | 454.328 | 482.4 |
| 25 | | | | | | | |
| 26 | | | | | | | |
| 27 **Real Resource Effects** | | | | | | | |
| 28 | | | | | | | |
| 29 | | | | | | | |
| 30 | –12.4 | –16.6 | –20.4 | –23.8 | –26.2 | –28.4 | –31 |
| 31 | –74 | –90 | –107 | –124 | –140 | –157 | –174 |
| 32 | | | | | | | |
| 33 | 1209 | 1423 | 1645 | 1882 | 2136 | 2404 | 2678 |
| 34 | | | | | | | |
| 35 | –12.09 | –14.23 | –16.45 | –18.82 | –21.36 | –24.04 | –26.78 |
| 36 | | | | | | | |
| 37 | **–110.58** | **–135.06** | **–160.3** | **–185.44** | **–208.92** | **–233.48** | **–258.56** |
| 38 | | | | | | | |
| 39 | –86.4 | –106.6 | –127.4 | –147.8 | –166.2 | –185.4 | –205 |

| 1 | **2002** | **2003** | **2004** | **2005** | **2006** | **2007** | **2008** |
|---|---|---|---|---|---|---|---|
| **PSBR Effects** | | | | | | | |
| 2 | –222 | –236 | –251 | –266 | –280 | –293 | –293 |
| 3 | –65 | –65 | –65 | –65 | –65 | –65 | –65 |
| 4 | 450 | 469 | 488 | 506 | 523 | 541 | 541 |
| 5 | –176 | –192 | –203 | –211 | –217 | –220 | –231 |
| 6 | **–13** | **–24** | **–31** | **–36** | **–39** | **–37** | **–48** |
| 7 | | | | | | | |
| 8 | | | | | | | |
| 9 | 450 | 469 | 488 | 506 | 523 | 541 | 541 |
| 10 | –211.2 | –230.4 | –243.6 | –253.2 | –260.4 | –264 | –277.2 |
| 11 | **–48.2** | **–62.4** | **–71.6** | **–78.2** | **–82.4** | **–81** | **–94.2** |
| 12 | | | | | | | |
| 13 | | | | | | | |
| 14 | 54 | 56.28 | 58.56 | 60.72 | 62.76 | 64.92 | 64.92 |
| 15 | –25.344 | –27.648 | –29.232 | –30.384 | –31.248 | –31.68 | –33.264 |
| 16 | **–258.344** | **–272.368** | **–286.672** | **–300.664** | **–313.488** | **–324.76** | **–326.344** |
| 17 | | | | | | | |
| 18 | | | | | | | |
| 19 | | | | | | | |
| 20 | 200 | 217 | 234 | 250 | 250 | 250 | 250 |
| 21 | **187** | **193** | **203** | **214** | **211** | **213** | **202** |
| 22 | **246.04** | **257.58** | **273.28** | **290.18** | **293.3** | **301.72** | **296.92** |
| 23 | | | | | | | |
| 24 | 504.384 | 529.948 | 559.952 | 590.844 | 606.788 | 626.48 | 623.264 |
| 25 | | | | | | | |
| 26 | | | | | | | |
| 27 **Real Resource Effects** | | | | | | | |
| 28 | | | | | | | |
| 29 | | | | | | | |
| 30 | –35.2 | –38.4 | –40.6 | –42.2 | –43.4 | –44 | –46.2 |
| 31 | –190 | –207 | –224 | –240 | –240 | –240 | –240 |
| 32 | | | | | | | |
| 33 | 2952 | 3229 | 3514 | 3809 | 4115 | 4436 | 4746 |
| 34 | | | | | | | |
| 35 | –29.52 | –32.29 | –35.14 | –38.09 | –41.15 | –44.36 | –47.46 |
| 36 | | | | | | | |
| 37 | **–284.24** | **–309.98** | **–334.88** | **–358.38** | **–365.7** | **–372.72** | **–381.12** |
| 38 | | | | | | | |
| 39 | –225.2 | –245.4 | –264.6 | –282.2 | –283.4 | –284 | –286.2 |

| 1 | 2009 | 2010 | 2011 | 2012 | 2013 | 2014 | 2015 |
|---|---|---|---|---|---|---|---|
| **PSBR Effects** | | | | | | | |
| 2 | –293 | –293 | –293 | –293 | –293 | –293 | –293 |
| 3 | –65 | –65 | –65 | –65 | –65 | –65 | –65 |
| 4 | 541 | 541 | 541 | 541 | 541 | 541 | 541 |
| 5 | –251 | –275 | –296 | –313 | –329 | –345 | –357 |
| 6 | **–68** | **–92** | **–113** | **–130** | **–146** | **–162** | **–174** |
| 7 | | | | | | | |
| 8 | | | | | | | |
| 9 | 541 | 541 | 541 | 541 | 541 | 541 | 541 |
| 10 | –301.2 | –330 | –355.2 | –375.6 | –394.8 | –414 | –428.4 |
| 11 | **–118.2** | **–147** | **–172.2** | **–192.6** | **–211.8** | **–231** | **–245.4** |
| 12 | | | | | | | |
| 13 | | | | | | | |
| 14 | 64.92 | 64.92 | 64.92 | 64.92 | 64.92 | 64.92 | 64.92 |
| 15 | –36.144 | –39.6 | –42.624 | –45.072 | –47.376 | –49.68 | –51.408 |
| 16 | **–329.224** | **–332.68** | **–335.704** | **–338.152** | **–340.436** | **–342.76** | **–344.488** |
| 17 | | | | | | | |
| 18 | | | | | | | |
| 19 | | | | | | | |
| 20 | 250 | 250 | 250 | 250 | 250 | 250 | 250 |
| 21 | **182** | **158** | **137** | **120** | **104** | **88** | **76** |
| 22 | **282.72** | **264.04** | **247.94** | **235.5** | **223.74** | **211.66** | **203.34** |
| 23 | | | | | | | |
| 24 | 611.944 | 596.72 | 583.644 | 573.652 | 564.196 | 554.42 | 547.828 |
| 25 | | | | | | | |
| 26 | | | | | | | |
| 27 **Real Resource Effects** | | | | | | | |
| 28 | | | | | | | |
| 29 | | | | | | | |
| 30 | –50.2 | –55 | –59.2 | –62.6 | –65.8 | –69 | –71.4 |
| 31 | –240 | –240 | –240 | –240 | –240 | –240 | –240 |
| 32 | | | | | | | |
| 33 | 5036 | 5302 | 5547 | 5775 | 5987 | 6183 | 6367 |
| 34 | | | | | | | |
| 35 | –50.36 | –53.02 | –55.47 | –57.75 | –59.87 | –61.83 | –63.67 |
| 36 | | | | | | | |
| 37 | **–390.92** | **–401.04** | **–410.14** | **–418.1** | **–425.54** | **–432.66** | **–438.74** |
| 38 | | | | | | | |
| 39 | –290.2 | –295 | –299.2 | –302.6 | –305.8 | –309 | –311.4 |

| 1 | **2016** | **2017** | **2018** | **2019** | **2020** | **2021** | **2022** |
|---|---|---|---|---|---|---|---|
| **PSBR Effects** | | | | | | | |
| 2 | –293 | –293 | –293 | –293 | –293 | –293 | –293 |
| 3 | –65 | –65 | –65 | –65 | –65 | –65 | –65 |
| 4 | 541 | 541 | 541 | 541 | 541 | 541 | 541 |
| 5 | –367 | –375 | –383 | –388 | –393 | –399 | –404 |
| 6 | **–184** | **–192** | **–200** | **–205** | **–210** | **–216** | **–221** |
| 7 | | | | | | | |
| 8 | | | | | | | |
| 9 | 541 | 541 | 541 | 541 | 541 | 541 | 541 |
| 10 | –440.4 | –450 | –459.6 | –465.6 | –471.6 | –478.8 | –484.8 |
| 11 | **–257.4** | **–267** | **–276.6** | **–282.6** | **–288.6** | **–295.8** | **–301.8** |
| 12 | | | | | | | |
| 13 | | | | | | | |
| 14 | 64.92 | 64.92 | 64.92 | 64.92 | 64.92 | 64.92 | 64.92 |
| 15 | –52.848 | –54 | –55.152 | –55.872 | –56.592 | –57.456 | –58.176 |
| 16 | **–345.928** | **–347.08** | **–348.232** | **–348.952** | **–349.672** | **–350.536** | **–351.256** |
| 17 | | | | | | | |
| 18 | | | | | | | |
| 19 | | | | | | | |
| 20 | 250 | 250 | 250 | 250 | 250 | 250 | 250 |
| 21 | **66** | **58** | **50** | **45** | **40** | **34** | **29** |
| 22 | **196.82** | **192.14** | **187.3** | **185.36** | **183.32** | **180.16** | **177.9** |
| 23 | | | | | | | |
| 24 | 542.748 | 539.22 | 535.532 | 534.312 | 532.992 | 530.696 | 529.156 |
| 25 | | | | | | | |
| 26 | | | | | | | |
| 27 **Real Resource Effects** | | | | | | | |
| 28 | | | | | | | |
| 29 | | | | | | | |
| 30 | –73.4 | –75 | –76.6 | –77.6 | –78.6 | –79.8 | –80.8 |
| 31 | –240 | –240 | –240 | –240 | –240 | –240 | –240 |
| 32 | | | | | | | |
| 33 | 6541 | 6707 | 6865 | 7018 | 7166 | 7308 | 7445 |
| 34 | | | | | | | |
| 35 | –65.41 | –67.07 | –68.65 | –70.18 | –71.66 | –73.08 | –74.45 |
| 36 | | | | | | | |
| 37 | **–444.22** | **–449.14** | **–453.9** | **–457.96** | **–461.92** | **–465.96** | **–469.7** |
| 38 | | | | | | | |
| 39 | –313.4 | –315 | –316.6 | –317.6 | –318.6 | –319.8 | –320.8 |

| 1 | 2023 | 2024 | 2025 | 2026 | 2027 |
|---|---|---|---|---|---|
| **PSBR Effects** | | | | | |
| 2 | –293 | –293 | –293 | –293 | –293 |
| 3 | –65 | –65 | –65 | –65 | –65 |
| 4 | 541 | 541 | 541 | 541 | 541 |
| 5 | –407 | –410 | –411 | –411 | –412 |
| 6 | **–224** | **–227** | **–228** | **–228** | **–229** |
| 7 | | | | | |
| 8 | | | | | |
| 9 | 541 | 541 | 541 | 541 | 541 |
| 10 | –488.4 | –492 | –493.2 | –493.2 | –494.4 |
| 11 | **–305.4** | **–309** | **–310.2** | **–310.2** | **–311.4** |
| 12 | | | | | |
| 13 | | | | | |
| 14 | 64.92 | 64.92 | 64.92 | 64.92 | 64.92 |
| 15 | –58.608 | –59.04 | –59.184 | –59.184 | –59.328 |
| 16 | **–351.688** | **–352.12** | **–352.264** | **–352.264** | **–354.408** |
| 17 | | | | | |
| 18 | | | | | |
| 19 | | | | | |
| 20 | 250 | 250 | 250 | 250 | 250 |
| 21 | **26** | **23** | **22** | **22** | **21** |
| 22 | **177.58** | **177.2** | **178.8** | **181.4** | **182.98** |
| 23 | | | | | |
| 24 | 529.268 | 529.32 | 531.064 | 533.664 | 535.388 |
| 25 | | | | | |
| 26 | | | | | |
| 27 **Real Resource Effects** | | | | | |
| 28 | | | | | |
| 29 | | | | | |
| 30 | –81.4 | –82 | –82.2 | –82.2 | –82.4 |
| 31 | –240 | –240 | –240 | –240 | –240 |
| 32 | | | | | |
| 33 | 7579 | 7710 | 7840 | 7970 | 8099 |
| 34 | | | | | |
| 35 | –75.79 | –77.1 | –78.4 | –79.7 | –80.99 |
| 36 | | | | | |
| 37 | **–472.98** | **–476.2** | **–479** | **–481.6** | **–484.38** |
| 38 | | | | | |
| 39 | –321.4 | –322 | –322.2 | –322.2 | –322.4 |

EXPLANATORY NOTES TO TABLE A1

**Lines 2-6** are taken directly from Annex E of the White Paper (UK, 1988, Cm 520). Line 6 is the PSBR effect shown in the White Paper, to which must be added £15 million per year for the Access Funds. Line 6 is shown graphically in Figure 3.

**Line 9** is the same as line 4.

**Line 10** = line 5 × 90/75. Line 10 is the White Paper repayment stream inflated by 20 per cent to reflect the fact that 90 per cent of repayments are collected, rather than 75 per cent.

**Line 11** = lines (2 + 3 + 9 + 10). This is the White Paper PSBR effect assuming a 10 per cent leakage rather than the White Paper's 25 per cent figure. Line 11 is shown graphically in Figure 4.

**Lines 14 and 15**: line 14 = 0.12 × line 9, and line 15 = 0.12 × line 10. Lines 14 and 15 reflect the assumption that only 12 per cent of net outstanding loans need to be guaranteed, and so only 12 per cent of the net outlays (i.e. gross outlays minus gross repayments) count as part of public spending.

**Line 16** = lines (2 + 3 + 14 + 15). This is the PSBR effect of the NIC scheme, with a 10 per cent leakage, and where students borrow from banks; banks receive a guarantee of up to 12 per cent of outstanding loans. Line 16 is shown graphically by the lowest line in Figure 5.

**Line 20**: administrative costs are assumed to rise in steps of £50 million every three years (see text), to a peak of £250 million.

**Line 21** = lines (6 + 20). Line 21 is the PSBR effect in the White Paper with the addition of administrative costs. It is shown in Figure 5 as the PSBR effect including administrative costs, but excluding the cost of the interest subsidy.

**Line 22** = line 21 minus (2 × line 35). Line 35 is the saving from reducing the interest on outstanding loans by 1 per cent. Line 22 shows the PSBR effect of the White Paper scheme including administrative costs and the cost of subsidising outstanding loans by 2 per cent. It is shown in Figure 5 as the PSBR effect including the interest subsidy.

**Line 24** = line 22 minus line 16. Line 24 shows the difference in the PSBR effects of the White Paper scheme and the NI scheme, taking account of the extra administrative costs, leakages and interest subsidy of the White Paper scheme. It is shown graphically as the difference between the top and bottom lines in Figure 5.

**Line 30** = 0.2 × line 5: see the explanation to line 10. Reducing leakages from 25 per cent to 10 per cent increases repayments by 20 per cent; the saving is thus 20 per cent of line 5.

**Line 31** = line 20 minus £10 million, i.e. it is assumed that the *extra* cost of administering NICs will be £10 million per year. Line 31 is shown as the first line below the zero axis in Figure 6, and the sum of lines 30 and 31 as the second line below the zero axis.

**Line 33** shows cumulative outstanding loans: thus outstanding loans in 1990 (see lines 4 and 5) are 167–0 = 167; in 1991 they are 167 + 193–2 = 358; in 1992 they are 167 + 193 + 216–2–9 = 565, etc.

**Line 35** = (–0.01) × line 33. I.e. line 35 = 1 per cent of cumulative outstanding loans; it is multiplied by minus one to show the saving because the subsidy is not needed in the NIC scheme. Line 35 shows the amount saved for each 1 per cent of interest subsidy which is avoided.

**Line 37** = lines (30 + 31) + (2 × line 35). Line 37 shows the total savings of the NIC scheme compared with the White Paper scheme via reduced leakages (line 30), lower administrative costs (line 31) and a 2 per cent lower interest subsidy (2 × line 35). Line 37 is shown as the lowest line in Figure 6.

**Line 39** = lines (30 + 31). Line 39 shows the savings of the NIC scheme compared with the White Paper scheme, ignoring interest subsidies.

# Appendix 2: The Time Path of Indexed Repayments

**The intuition of indexed repayments** at first glance appears paradoxical; but the puzzle can be resolved.

Chapter 5.2 argues that an indexed loan of £1000 can be repaid over 25 years at a 2 per cent interest rate by an extra National Insurance Contribution (NIC) of 0.33p, assuming real earnings of £12,000 per year. The loan is taken out in real terms (i.e. adjusted so as to exclude the effects of inflation) and repaid in real terms. Doing the calculations in nominal terms must logically give the same result. Suppose a student borrowed £4000. An extra NIC of 1.33 pence, at earnings of £12,000 yields £160. However, if the nominal interest rate is seven per cent (e.g. 5 per cent inflation plus 2 per cent interest) then the nominal interest payment would be £280 (7 per cent of £4000). It looks as though the repayment in Chapter 5.2 does not cover interest charges, and so indebtedness rises.

The nominal calculation below shows that this is indeed the case. Nominal repayments in the early years do not fully cover interest charges and inflation, so nominal debt rises. Eventually, however, repayments start to rise rapidly in nominal terms and the nominal debt falls. The intuition, on reflection, is clear. Typical mortgage arrangements (which are not indexed) impose a back breaking cost in the early years; in later years inflation erodes the real debt and real earnings rise, so that repayment can become trivial. Indexing the loan makes it possible to charge a lower interest rate. The method makes use of the *de facto* indexation of earnings to equalise real repayments over the duration of the loan; thus repayments are smaller than a conventional loan early on, and larger later.

It is precisely because an indexed loan avoids the huge front-end loading of conventional mortgages that early repayments fail to cover interest in full. Were it otherwise, there would be no front-end relief. Matters are rectified in later years as real earnings rise.

**Calculation** I am grateful to Mark Robson for the following Basic programme, which sets out the calculation of an indexed loan. It is assumed (for simplicity) that inflation is 5 per cent per year, that real earnings rise by 2 per cent a year, and that the real interest charge is 2 per cent. In Table A2, the student borrows £1000; his earnings in year 1 are assumed to be £12,000 and his first year repayment is £40 (i.e. 0.33 per cent of £12,000, taken from Table 2). In each subsequent year repayment is £40 written up by the interest factor in column (1), which takes account of inflation (5 per cent) and interest (2 per cent).

```
dim o(30)
dim d(30)
o(0)=1000
d(0)=1000
N=25: r=0.02: pi=0.05

for i=1 to N
o(i)=o(i–1)*(1+r+pi)–o(0)/N*(1+r+pi)^i
d(i)=d(i–1)–d(0)/N
lprint using "££££.££";i,(1+r+pi)^i,o(i)

end
```

In the programme, o(i) is the outstanding nominal debt in year i, shown in column (2) of Table A2. Column (1) shows the effect of compound interest at a nominal interest rate of 7 per cent per year. Column (2) shows clearly how the nominal debt rises in the early years, reaches a peak (in this example in year 10), and then starts to decline. In purely nominal terms the debt does not fall below the initial £1000 borrowed until year 18. By year 25 the indexed loan is fully paid off, as stated in Chapter 5.2.

TABLE A2: NOMINAL INDEBTEDNESS WITH INDEXED REPAYMENTS

| YEAR | INTEREST FACTOR (1) | OUTSTANDING NOMINAL DEBT (2) |
|---|---|---|
| 1 | 1.07 | 1027.20 |
| 2 | 1.14 | 1053.31 |
| 3 | 1.23 | 1078.04 |
| 4 | 1.31 | 1101.07 |
| 5 | 1.40 | 1122.04 |
| 6 | 1.50 | 1140.56 |
| 7 | 1.61 | 1156.16 |
| 8 | 1.72 | 1168.37 |
| 9 | 1.84 | 1176.61 |
| 10 | 1.97 | 1180.29 |
| 11 | 2.10 | 1178.72 |
| 12 | 2.25 | 1171.14 |
| 13 | 2.41 | 1156.73 |
| 14 | 2.58 | 1134.55 |
| 15 | 2.76 | 1103.61 |
| 16 | 2.95 | 1062.78 |
| 17 | 3.16 | 1010.82 |
| 18 | 3.38 | 946.38 |
| 19 | 3.62 | 867.97 |
| 20 | 3.87 | 773.94 |
| 21 | 4.14 | 662.49 |
| 22 | 4.43 | 531.65 |
| 23 | 4.74 | 379.24 |
| 24 | 5.07 | 202.89 |
| 25 | 5.43 | 0.00 |

# Notes

**Chapter 1,** pp 1 to 15

1 It is a standard proposition in econometrics that omitted independent variables, unless they are orthogonal to the included variables, will cause biased ordinary least squares estimators. Similar problems generally arise with maximum likelihood estimation.

2 As a piece of casual empiricism, LSE graduates by no means always go on to vast salaries; but they do, disproportionately, end up in jobs which they enjoy.

3 Higher-education institutions can perhaps be likened to firms as analysed by Cyert and March (1963); they discuss firms whose managers do not seek to maximise profit, but seek to maximise their own utility subject to a profit constraint.

4 Quoted by Robert Jackson, the Minister for Higher Education, on BBC Radio 4's *Analysis*, 3 November 1988.

**Chapter 2,** pp 16 to 20

1 For a brief, official description of current institutions, see UK, 1988, Annex A.

2 The figures include contributions by the students themselves; see UK, 1988, para 2.4.

3 Robert Jackson in evidence to the House of Commons Select Committee on Education, 14 December 1988; see also UK, 1988, para 2.25.

4 Kenneth Baker, when introducing the White Paper on top-up loans said that the Labour Shadow Education Secretary was 'defending the indefensible. He is defending a system that has actually restricted access to higher education' (*Hansard* (Commons), 9 November 1988, col 307).

5 The extent to which parental contributions rise with income emerges clearly in Figures 2A, B and C, as discussed in Chapter 3.1.

**Chapter 3,** pp 21 to 31

1 The figures in UK (1988, Annex C, Charts A and B) on which the analysis is based are all in purchasing power parity terms.

2 Under the so-called Ryrie rules any sum guaranteed by the Treasury has to be added *in full* to public expenditure; the topic is discussed in detail in Chapter 4.4.

3 The US Perkins Loan Program has a 13 per cent default rate (UK, 1988, Annex C, para 10), a figure which is not untypical. For more detailed discussion, see Johnstone (1986, Ch 6) and Underwood (1989). For up-to-the-minute accounts, see 'Huge Losses Put US Loan System at Risk', *Times Higher Education Supplement*, 17 March 1989, p 11, and 'Quote . . . Unquote', *The Guardian*, 20 March 1989, p 23. The *Guardian* article reproduces a report in the *Washington Post* of a 20 per cent default rate for student loans from the US government.

**Chapter 4,** pp 32 to 51

1 Though the main body of the White Paper is heavily criticised, the Annexes contain much interesting and useful material.
2 At the end of the tax year every employee receives a P60 form from his/her employer showing his/her total earnings and tax payments over the year just finished.
3 Royal Academy of Dramatic Art; actors are only one example of a profession with wildly fluctuating incomes.
4 When someone changes job the Inland Revenue sends a P45 form to his/her new employer, giving details of the individual's tax code and previous earnings.
5 The 'lump' consists largely of self-employed building workers, a notorious source of tax evasion.
6 See the Glossary.
7 See the Glossary.
8 The figure is calculated by adding the public-expenditure costs in Annex E of the White Paper (line (1) of Table 1), and adding £15 million each year, which is expenditure on the three Access Funds (UK, 1988, paras 3.21–3.25).

**Chapter 5,** pp 52 to 66

1 See the Glossary.
2 Thus the moral hazard problem associated with mortgage-type loans (i.e. the incentive they give borrowers to default) is avoided.
3 No National Insurance Contributions are levied below the lower earnings limit (see the Glossary). As a result of the changes in the March 1989 Budget, once that limit is exceeded, NICs are payable at 2 per cent of *total* earnings below the lower earnings limit (£43 per week in 1989/90). An increase in earnings from £42.99 to £43.01 therefore makes the individual liable for NICs of 86 pence (i.e. 2 per cent of £43), thus facing him/her with a 'spike'. Earnings in excess of £43 per week pay NICs at 9p in the pound. Thus for weekly earnings of £43 per week or more, an individual's NIC is 86 pence plus 9 per cent of earnings above £43.
4 Treasury officials in private have confirmed that there is no case for applying the Ryrie rules to total student borrowing, but at most to that proportion which is guaranteed.
5 Mortgage Interest Relief at Source: under MIRAS I pay my Building Society £75 for each £100 in interest I owe; the Building Society receives the remaining £25 directly from the tax authorities. Thus there is no need to change a person's tax code if the mortgage interest rate changes.
6 An individual who works in the home looking after young children or the disabled is automatically entitled to home responsibility protection, whereby he/she is 'credited' with National Insurance contributions. Thus years for which home responsibility protection is received count as full contribution years for entitlement to benefits such as the National Insurance Retirement Pension.

# Glossary

**DES:** Department of Education and Science.

**DSS:** Department of Social Security.

**Lower Earnings Limit** for National Insurance: individuals with earnings below the Lower Earnings Limit (£43 per week in 1989/90) pay no National Insurance Contributions.

**NICs:** National Insurance Contributions, levied at a rate of 9 per cent of earnings for most employed persons.

**Option A** in the White Paper refers to loans with mortgage-type repayments.

**Option D** in the White Paper refers to loans with income-related repayments.

**PAYE:** Pay-As-You-Earn, the UK system of withholding income tax by employers.

**PSBR:** Public Sector Borrowing Requirement.

**SERPS:** State Earnings Related Pension Scheme.

**Upper Earnings Limit** for National Insurance: once an individual's income has reached the Upper Earnings Limit (£325 per week in 1989/90) no additional National Insurance Contribution is levied.

# References


Akerlof, G A (1970), 'The Market for "Lemons": Qualitative Uncertainty and the Market Mechanism', *Quarterly Journal of Economics,* Vol 84, pp 488–500, August.

Barnes, A J L, and Barr, N A (1988), *Strategies for Higher Education: The Alternative White Paper,* Aberdeen University Press for the David Hume Institute and the Suntory-Toyota International Centre for Economics and Related Disciplines, London School of Economics.

Barr, N A (1977), 'PAYE Codes in 1977–8', *British Tax Review,* No 6.

Barr, N A (1987), *The Economics of the Welfare State,* London: Weidenfeld and Nicolson.

Barr, N A (1989), *Student Support: An Analysis and International Comparison,* (forthcoming).

Barr, N A and Low, W (1988), *Student Grants and Student Poverty,* London School of Economics, Welfare State Programme, Discussion Paper No 28.

Blaug, M (1966), 'Loans for Students', *New Society,* 6 October, pp 538–9.

Blaug, M (1967), 'Approaches to Educational Planning, *Economic Journal,* June.

Blaug, M (1970), *An Introduction to the Economics of Education*, London: Penguin.

Blaug, M (1976), 'The Empirical Status of Human Capital Theory: A Slightly Jaundiced Survey', *Journal of Economic Literature,* September, pp 827–56.

Blaug, M (1980), 'Student Loans and the NUS', *Economic Affairs,* October, pp 45–6.

Buiter, W H (1985), 'A Guide to Public Sector Debt and Deficits', *Economic Policy,* November.

Conservative Party (1987), *The Next Moves Forward.*

Cornish, J W P and Windle, R E (1988), *Undergraduate Income and Expenditure Survey 1986–7,* London: Research Services Limited.

Dahrendorf, R (1988), *The Modern Social Conflict,* London: Weidenfeld and Nicolson.

Friedman, M (1976), *Price Theory*, Chicago: Aldine Publishing Company.

Glennerster, H, Merrett, S, and Wilson, G (1968), 'A Graduate Tax', *Higher Education Review*, Vol 1, No 1.

Goodin, R E and Le Grand, J (eds) (1987), *Not Only the Poor: The Middle Classes and the Welfare State,* London: Allen and Unwin.

Gordon, A (1981), 'The Educational Choices of Young People', in O Fulton (ed), *Access to Higher Education*, Leverhulme Programme of Study into the Future of Higher Education.

Johansson, O and Ricknell, L (1985), *Study Assistance in Ten European Countries,* Umea University.

Johnson, C (1989), 'Student Loans: A Better Way', *Lloyds Bank Economic Bulletin*, No 122, February.

Johnstone, D B (1986), *Sharing the Costs of Higher Education*, New York: College Entrance Examination Board.

Kedourie, E (1988), *Diamonds into Glass*, London: Centre for Policy Studies.

Layard, P R G (1972), 'Economic Theories of Educational Planning', in Peston, M, and Corry, B (eds), *Essays in Honour of Lord Robbins*, London: Weidenfeld and Nicolson.

Layard, P R G, and Walters, A A (1978), *Microeconomic Theory*, London: McGraw-Hill.

Le Grand, J (1984), 'Equity as an Economic Objective', *Journal of Applied Philosophy*, Vol 1, No 1, pp 39–51.

Le Grand, J and Robinson, R (1984), *The Economics of Social Problems*, 2nd edn, London: Macmillan.

Marshall, A (1961), *Principles of Economics*, 9th edn, London: Macmillan.

Moser, C A, and Layard, P R G (1964), 'Planning the Scale of Higher Education in Britain: Some Statistical Problems', *Journal of the Royal Statistical Society*, December, pp 473–513, and Discussion, *ibid.*, pp 513–26.

Peacock, A T, and Wiseman, J (1964), *Education for Democrats*, London: Institute on Economic Affairs.

Prest, A R (1966), *Financing University Education*, London: Institute of Economic Affairs.

Robbins, L C (1980), *Higher Education Revisited*, London: Macmillan.

Sherlock, M (1988), 'Baker's Loans', *The Guardian*, 15 November 1988, p 27.

Spence, M (1973), 'Job Market Signalling', *Quarterly Journal of Economics*, Vol 87, August, pp 355–74.

UK (1960), *Grants to Students* (the Anderson Report), Report of the Committee Appointed by the Minister of Education and the Secretary of State for Scotland, Cmnd 1051, London: HMSO.

UK (1963), *Higher Education* (the Robbins Report), Cmnd 2154, London: HMSO.

UK (1985), *The Development of Higher Education into the 1990s*, Cmnd 9524, London: HMSO.

UK (1988), *Top-Up Loans for Students*, Cm 520, London: HMSO.

Underwood, S (1989), *Student Financial Aid in the United States and Its Lessons for the United Kingdom*, University of York.

Varian, H R (1984), *Microeconomic Analysis*, 2nd edn, New York: Norton.

Williams, G, and Gordon, A (1981), 'Perceived Earnings Functions and ex ante Rates of Return to Post Compulsory Education in England', *Higher Education*, Vol 10, No 2, pp 199–227.

Woodhall, M (1983*a*), 'The Links between Finance and Admissions Policies in Higher Education', *Policies for Higher Education in the 1980s*, Paris: OECD.

Woodhall, M (1983*b*), *Student Loans as a Means of Financing Higher Education: Lessons from International Experience*, Washington DC: The World Bank.

## SUNTORY TOYOTA INTERNATIONAL CENTE FOR ECONOMICS AND RELATED DISCIPLINES

ST/ICERD was established in 1978 on the basis of funds donated to the London School of Economics by Suntory Ltd. and the Toyota Motor Company Limited of Japan. It is the largest research centre at LSE, acting as a "research council" within the School, awarding funds on the basis of competitive peer review to finance a wide variety of research by members of the School staff, both inside and outside the Centre. It also provides funds for the LSE Suntory-Toyota public lectures and a variety of seminars in different fields. It produces discussion papers on a wide variety of subjects which are distributed free of charge. Eleven Occasional Papers have been produced to date, which are for sale from the Centre. Support for postgraduate students is offered annually in the form of studentships. In addition, the Centre is host to academic visitors from all over the world, and provides accommodation and facilities for research programmes supported by the ESRC and other funding agencies.

### OCCASIONAL PAPERS

1 The Economics of the Professions (1982) by Patrick Foley, Avner Shaked, John Sutton
A guide to the literature with over 100 items, with introductory essay and full cross references

2 Panel Data on Incomes (1983) Edited by A B Atkinson and F A Cowell
A selection of papers presented at a Conference held in June, 1982 on the Analysis of Panel Data on Incomes

3 Confucianism and Taoism (1984) by Max Weber, abridged by M Morishima. Translated by M Alter and J Hunter
A new translation of Weber's treatise on Chinese religions

4 Homeless in London, 1971–81 (1984) by Helen Austerberry, Kerry Schott, Sophie Watson
An analysis of the impact of the severe housing crisis in London — arising from the cutback in housing expenditure — on the different types of households most affected by it

5 Regionalisation in France, Italy and Spain (1984) Edited by M Hebbert and H Machin
Papers arising from a seminar held in June 1983 on nation–region conflicts in economic policy-making

6 Unemployment Benefits and Unemployment Duration (1985) by A B Atkinson and J Micklewright
Drawing on a sample of unemployed men in the UK in the 1970s, this study challenges the popular perception that the benefit system provides generous insurance and other support.
7 The Economics of Soviet Arms (1985) by Peter Wiles and Moshe Efrat
Part I is concerned with military expenditures in domestic rubles; Part II is about the economics of the Soviet Arms trade with the Third World
8 The Evolution of Central Banks (1985) by C A E Goodhart
This book seeks to establish, using analytical arguments and historical example, how the evolution of Central Banks occurred, and how far it was a natural development in response to revealed needs
9 Paying for Pensions: the French Experience (1985) by Tony Lynes
This study traces the history of developments in France's pension provision, culminating in the government's decision to reduce the pension age from 65 to 60 in 1983
10 Tax Benefit Models (1987) Edited by A B Atkinson and H Sutherland
This is a collection of papers describing the research underlying the construction of tax-benefit models, with illustrations of their use.
11 How Tokyo Grows: Land Development and Planning on the Metropolitan Fringe (1988) by Michael Hebbert and Norihiro Nakal
An analysis of the mechanisms of urban land development in Japan and a review of current policy measures

The Centre also produces discussion papers in the following subjects: Economics, Theoretical Economics, International Economics, Econometrics, International Studies, Japanese Studies, Comparative Industrial Relations and Information Technology. These are all available, free of charge, from Ruth Singh, (Room R411, 01-405-7686 ext. 3025).